How to Know God Exists

Scientific Proof of God

Ray Comfort

16pt

Copyright Page from the Original Book

How to Know God Exists: Scientific Proof of God

Published by:
Bridge-Logos
Alachua, Florida 32615, USA
www.bridgelogos.com

© 2007 by Ray Comfort. All rights reserved. No part of this publication may be reproduced, stored in a retrieval system, or transmitted by any means—electronic, mechanical, photographic (photocopy), recording, or otherwise—without written permission from the publisher.

Edited by Lynn Copeland

Cover, page design, and production by Genesis Group (www.genesis-group.net)

Printed in the United States of America

Library of Congress Number: 2012940603

ISBN: 978-0-88270-432-6

Unless otherwise indicated, Scripture quotations are from the *New King James* version, ©1979, 1980, 1982 by Thomas Nelson Inc., Publishers, Nashville, Tennessee.

TABLE OF CONTENTS

1: ARE ATHEISTS SMARTER THAN MOST?	1
2: ABSURD IN THE HIGHEST DEGREE	16
3: IS EVOLUTION SCIENTIFIC?	33
4: THE ORIGIN OF SPECIES	51
5: MUTANT TURTLES	61
6: SCIENCE AND ATHEISM	75
7: EVOLUTION'S STRANGE DILEMMA	92
8: THE FOUR GIFTS	107
9: THREE WISE FOOLS	119
10: THIS DAY WAS DIFFERENT	126
11: ALLEGED MISTAKES IN THE BIBLE	144
12: COMMON OBJECTIONS TO CHRISTIANITY	162
13: CONFESSIONS OF A ROCKET SCIENTIST	182
14: WHY BOTHER?	196
END NOTES	213
RESOURCES	226
BACK COVER MATERIAL	232

*"Only two things are infinite,
the universe and human stupidity,
and I'm not sure about the former."*

—Albert Einstein

Special thanks to Jennifer West, Anita Alvarado, and especially to my friend and faithful editor, Lynn Copeland

1

ARE ATHEISTS SMARTER THAN MOST?

"I do not feel obliged to believe that the same God who has endowed us with sense, reason, and intellect has intended us to forgo their use."

—Galileo Galilei

I have an encouraging wife. She was made for Comfort. It was November 2007, and the following month I was going to turn 58. As I was about to get into bed, I looked into the mirror at my shirtless physique and consoled myself with the words, "Could be worse." Sue quietly mumbled, "Not much..."

The way she said those words reminded me of the time I was running toward the back door of our house and hit my arm on the corner of a wall. I often do that sort of thing. (If I take out a hammer, Sue gets a Band-Aid ready.) As I lay on the floor and writhed in pain for a few minutes, I could hear my youngest son (then in his late teens) working in the garage. Just because hurting myself is an almost daily occurrence, it was no reason for him to take no notice, so I said, "Daniel, how come you didn't come out to see if I was okay? For all you know I could have hit my head and gone insane." He quietly mumbled, "How would we have known?"

I once spent the afternoon with a couple whose church I was to speak at that night. After a relaxing time in their living room, just before we left for the meeting I decided I would use their bathroom. I walked across the living room to the door, and casually opened it to find the man's wife standing at the end of the bed *in her underwear*. There was a scream like you've never heard. Then I pulled myself together, stopped screaming, apologized and closed the door. Unfortunately for me, the bathroom door and bedroom door were identical and side-by-side. I had opened the wrong one. Welcome to a day in the life of Ray Comfort.

So, you are holding a book written by a klutz. How then could a klutz put forward a serious case about, arguably, the most significant subject in the world: the existence of God? Whatever the answer, I want you to know that despite being the way I am, I take the issue that we are going to look at *very* seriously. This is because of the implications. If there is no God, then we can do as we please. We can eat, drink, and be party animals like there's no tomorrow. All that really matters is pleasure, and pleasure is okay as long as no one gets hurt in its pursuit.

However, if there is a God, and we are morally responsible to Him, then we have a problem. A big one. A problem that's more serious than a heart attack, because its consequences are eternal.

So, with those few thoughts in mind, let's look at the evidence for the existence of God.

Mr. Joe Average

First, imagine with me a day in the life of Joe Average, a typical atheist or agnostic. Perhaps you can identify with him. Joe doesn't think about creation, let alone the Creator. If you asked him if God had ever done anything for him, he probably couldn't think of one thing.

He gets out of bed early in the morning in his beachfront home, makes some toast, and without much thought spreads on some butter and honey. He then walks outside, takes a deep breath of the cool morning air and exhales slowly. He enjoys a glass of cold milk as he surveys his rose garden, listening to the birds chirping at the break of another day. He smiles, because as he looks toward the ocean he sees that rain is on its way. That means he won't have to water his garden. It's just another typical day for Joe Average.

Not quite. There is nothing "average" or mundane about Joe or what he has done that morning. He's actually a miracle machine that no manmade mechanism could even begin to imitate.

Recently, brilliant Japanese scientists created an amazing robot. It was amazing because it looked so human, and could even move somewhat like a human. There were a few obvious differences from *Homo sapiens* though. It wasn't alive, and it couldn't think, see, hear, touch, taste, or smell. Despite this, it was a marvel of human technology—the very best we can do at this moment in history.

There were a few other things the robot couldn't do. It couldn't run, walk, or even stand on its own two feet. Scientists had to hold it upright, because they didn't know how to create feet that balance an upright body of that size, let alone walk and run. Human feet are far too complex in design to imitate. With 26 bones; 33 joints; more than 100 muscles, tendons, and ligaments; and a network of blood vessels, nerves, skin, and soft tissue, the foot and ankle components work together to provide the body with support, balance, and mobility. However, Joe had no problem standing upright and walking, because his extraordinary feet were designed and created by God.

The "run-of-the-mill" piece of toast he made wasn't ordinary either. The bread was ground from wheat, which grew in the soil. God created soil containing nutrients that fed the wheat kernel, so it could mature into the wheat plant, which then produced more wheat kernels. When the kernels were harvested, they were ground into flour and mixed with yeast to make bread, so that Joe would have something to eat to satisfy his God-given appetite, giving him nutritional energy for the day.

The butter that he spread on the toast came from milk that came from a cow that chewed grass that came from soil nutrients that God created.

The honey he enjoyed was produced by an insect that God created to collect nectar from flowers that grew from the soil that He had made.

As Joe gazed at his garden and inhaled deeply, he breathed in life-giving oxygen that had been released by trees that God had made. He then breathed out carbon dioxide, giving the trees what they depend on for their survival.

The milk Joe drank helped him satisfy the recurring thirst God had created within him, causing him to want to drink to keep his body properly hydrated. The refreshing liquid came from the cow that chewed the grass that came from the soil that God had made.

Joe looked at his yard using his amazing God-given eyes, with their millions of light-sensitive cells and incredible self-focusing muscles, which sent the images to his brain. There they were interpreted, enabling him to see his garden, filled with colorful flowers, waiting for the bees to come and get nectar to make honey for his toast.

With his astoundingly made ears, he listened to the variety of chirping birds, as they welcomed a new day and sung praises to Him who created all things.

It began to rain, and as the drops fell through the atmosphere, the sunlight shining through the transparent liquid splayed out into the seven colors of the rainbow. The sun's rays are traveling at 186,000 miles per second in a perfectly straight line, until they are refracted into myriad directions by that tiny, fast-moving water drop.

When the little drop hits the ocean surface, it sends out tiny waves in a perfect circle, as its energy is absorbed into the vast ocean.

The water surface looks flat to Joe's unaided eye, but over the horizon, the seemingly flat ocean curves to his left and right, as well as in front of him, and on the other side of the earth it turns upside down. Yet it doesn't spill into space because of the same law of gravity God created that pulled the drop from the great cloud to water Mr. Average's garden. This is all happening as Joe stands on this huge ball of dirt we call Earth, which is spinning around, as well as moving through space at 67,000mph.

As the Bible so rightly observes of the wonders of God's creation, "He did not leave Himself without witness, in that He did good, gave us rain from heaven and fruitful seasons, filling our hearts with food and gladness" (Acts 14:17). Yet despite this evidence, Joe can't think of a single thing that God has ever done for him.

Do you believe there is a God who made all these things? If not, then *you* create a cow that can chew green grass and make white milk that can turn into yellow butter. *You* make an eye, an ear, or a brain. Just make one ... from nothing. Or make a living flower that can produce nectar that can be collected by bees that you made, and have them transform it into honey for you to eat. Or create one drop of water from nothing and cause the sun's rays to split into seven colors. And since atheists believe that all this came about without an intelligent guiding force—there was no "mind" behind creation—imagine that I removed your brain and *then* asked you to do this. It would be absurd to believe that could happen.

In fact, the majority of people have a hard time believing that this amazing complexity of life is pure happenstance. It turns out that Mr. Joe Average isn't so average after all. According to a 2007 *Newsweek* poll, 91 percent of U.S. adults say they believe in God.[1] What do they see that Joe doesn't? Are they all merely imagining a Creator who isn't there? Are the 3 percent of Americans who claim to be atheists just smarter than most people ... or are they missing some obvious evidence?

> *Are the 3 percent of Americans who claim to be atheists just smarter than most people ... or are they missing some obvious evidence?*

An atheist is defined as one who believes there is no God. Since it isn't possible to prove scientifically that something *doesn't* exist, atheists cannot *know* that there is no God. Their view is just a belief based on lack of evidence. However, *believing* that there is no God does not mean that there isn't one. If there is a God, your eternity rests on your belief, so it's vital that you back it up with verifiable facts.

As mentioned earlier, "He did not leave Himself without witness." God wants us to know Him. The evidence is there, and God's existence can be proved.

The Sciences

To approach this subject scientifically, you will need to keep an open mind as you read through these pages. After all, in science, no theory is considered absolute truth.[2] Scientists are constantly revising and refining their theories as new information comes to light. All I ask is that you do the same: be willing to discard old ideas as you consider the evidence that is presented.

To begin our look at the scientific proof of God's existence, let's review the different sciences. They can be divided into:
- Physical sciences
- Earth sciences
- Life sciences

These are called "pure" sciences, in contrast to the "applied" or "engineering" sciences (technology), which are concerned with the practical application of scientific findings.
- The *physical sciences* focus on the nature and behavior of matter and energy. In physics, scientists study the relationships among energy, force, matter, and time in an attempt to explain how these shape the physical behavior of the universe.
- The *earth sciences* examine the structure and composition of our planet, and the physical processes that have helped to shape it.
- The *life sciences* (biology) study the development, distribution, function, origin, and structure of living things.

It's evident from the above that "science" focuses on, examines, and studies creation, giving us knowledge about our world. The word "scientific" originates from the Latin word *scientificus,* which means "producing knowledge." So what would constitute "scientific" proof of God?

To prove God's existence scientifically, we could look at the "anthropic principle." This principle is derived from the very delicate balance of conditions necessary for human life. Or we could look at the fascinating subjects of cosmology, biochemistry, entropy, relativity, and quantum mechanics.

While there are many intriguing topics we could explore to find evidences for God (some of which we'll cover in later chapters), for now we are going to confine ourselves to what the Greeks called "beautiful simplicity." We will simply be "producing knowledge" by applying basic logic to three clear evidences for the existence of God. We will do this knowing full well that this simplicity may be offensive to some who profess wisdom.

I hope you are not disappointed, in case you were expecting God to be produced in a Petri dish. Instead, we will be looking at the following three ways we can know that God exists:
- Intellectual knowledge
- Subconscious knowledge
- Experiential knowledge

Since science is the study of our natural world, for the first "scientific" (knowledge-producing) evidence of God, we'll look at creation itself.

Millions of Years

I would like to begin by sharing a simple analogy that I have used for many years as a tongue-in-cheek illustration for the existence of God. This is my theory of where the Coca-Cola can may have come from.

Billions of years ago, there was a massive explosion in space. Nobody knows what caused the big bang, it just happened, and from the explosion issued a massive rock, and on top of that rock was found a sweet, brown, bubbly substance.

Over millions of years, aluminum crept up the side and formed itself into a can, then into a lid, and eventually a tab. And millions of years later, red and white paints fell from the sky and formed themselves into the words "Coca-Cola, 12 fluid ounces."

You may rightly say, "What are you talking about? You are insulting my intellect." You know that if the soda can has been made, there *must* be a maker. If it was designed, there *must* be a designer. To believe it happened by sheer chance—created out of nothing—is to move into an intellectual-free zone.

This parody of evolutionary theory illustrates how silly it is. Yet this is exactly what evolutionists claim: something can bring itself into being from nothing, and with enough time, complex systems can be assembled by chance through random, unguided processes. We intuitively know when something is designed, and we know that things don't design and create themselves. For some reason, we understand this logic for every subject except our incredible creation—with its amazing design, complexity, beauty, and order. That just doesn't make sense.

If the first man to walk on the moon had uncovered a Coke can on its surface, would it be reasonable to surmise that it had evolved there over millions of years? Or would you know it was designed and created, and therefore someone must have been there before? Now think about how simplistic the Coke can is compared to the design, beauty, order, and complexity of our marvelous creation!

On our television program, "The Way of the Master," after using the Coke can example I held up a banana and jokingly called it "the atheist's nightmare." I explained how it was shaped for the human hand, had a tab, a wrapper, etc., comparing it to the Coke can to show obvious "design." Although my co-host, Kirk Cameron, gently warned me that atheists would take it out of context and make me look like a fool, we went ahead and used the clip anyway. But Kirk was right. Atheists didn't find the humor in it. They made a monkey out of me by taking the clip out of context and posting it on the Internet, saying a banana was the best proof I had for the existence of God. It isn't, of course. But I'd rather risk someone making a monkey out of me for presenting evidence of God, than to have scientists make monkeys out of all of us by claiming that we're related when we're not. In these pages I'll present more evidence than just a banana, so you can decide for yourself whether I've made my case.

Consider what two of the greatest scientific minds in history have said about the evidence of design in creation:

> This most beautiful system of the sun, planets, and comets, could only proceed

from the counsel and dominion of an intelligent and powerful Being.[3]
—Sir Isaac Newton

In view of such harmony in the cosmos which I, with my limited human mind, am able to recognize, there are yet people who say there is no God. But what makes me really angry is that they quote me for support of such views.[4]
—Albert Einstein

While Einstein didn't believe in a personal God, he didn't consider himself to be an atheist or even a pantheist. In reference to God, he said, "I want to know His thoughts." That's not the talk of pantheism. He also said, "We are in the position of a little child entering a huge library filled with books in many different languages. The child knows someone must have written those books. It does not know how. The child dimly suspects a mysterious order in the arrangement of the books but doesn't know what it is. That, it seems to me, is the attitude of even the most intelligent human being toward God. We see a universe marvelously arranged and obeying certain laws, but only dimly understand these laws. Our limited minds cannot grasp the mysterious force that moves the constellations."[5]

Friedrich Dürrenmatt said of him, "Einstein used to speak of God so often that I almost looked upon him as a disguised theologian."[6] The great genius once said, "The deeper one penetrates into nature's secrets, the greater becomes one's respect for God."[7] To one of the world's greatest scientists, the order and design in creation give evidence of God.

It's really *very* simple. When I look at a building, what proof is there that there was a builder? I can't see him, hear him, touch, taste, or smell him.

The building is absolute, 100 percent scientific proof that there was a builder. You cannot have a building without a builder. I don't need faith to believe in a builder; all I need is eyes that can see and a brain that works.

This same principle works for paintings and painters. Think of the Mona Lisa. When I look at the painting, how can I know there was a painter? Isn't it true—the painting is absolute, 100 percent scientific proof that there was a painter? You couldn't want better proof that there was a painter than to have the painting in front of you. I don't need faith to believe in a painter. All I need is eyes that can see and a brain that works.

Exactly the same applies with the existence of God. How can we know that a Creator exists? You can't see Him, hear Him, touch, taste, or smell Him. The logical, undeniable answer is that creation is absolute, 100 percent scientific proof that there was a Creator.

Some may claim that we can logically conclude there is a builder or painter only because we've observed people creating buildings and paintings. But if someone from the heart of a primitive jungle arrived in New York City, never having seen a high-rise, should he then conclude that none of the buildings in the city had a builder, because he had never seen one being built? I'm certain the most primitive of natives wouldn't come to such a ridiculous conclusion. But even if he did believe that they all sprang up by accident, his belief wouldn't change the reality that every building in New York City had a builder.

You cannot have a creation without a Creator. I don't need faith to believe in a Creator; all I need is eyes that can see and a brain that works.

2

ABSURD IN THE HIGHEST DEGREE

"All I have seen teaches me to trust the Creator for all I have not seen."

—Ralph Waldo Emerson

As we considered in the previous chapter, all paintings have painters. No sane person has ever claimed to find a painting that had no painter. Nor has there ever been a building discovered that didn't have a builder. We applied this same simple logic to creation. Everything created has a creator. That is just common sense. There's nothing complicated about it; a child can understand such logic. So, let's continue with this "beautiful simplicity" as we consider where mankind came from.

Could I ever convince you that my car had no maker? Let's say I ask you if you like my car. You reply, "Yes, what make is it?" and I say, "Oh, it didn't have a maker. It fell together in our backyard ... took millions of years."

You would probably respond with annoyance, "Come on, what make is it?" because you can see that it's been "made" with purpose in mind. It has a windshield for you to see where you are going. It has tiny squirters to lubricate the wind shield, and windshield wipers to keep the glass clean.

Think of the human body. Are you any less designed? In a similar way, you have "windshields" so that you can see where you are going. They are not simply a couple of marbles in the slots of your head. I want to take the time to show how fearfully and wonderfully we are made by giving some details of the composition of the eye, the ear, and the nose—body parts we all seem to take for granted ... until something goes wrong with them.

Please be patient with me as I get a little technical. I want to put some of these thoughts under a microscope to see the incredible nature of creation, so that we will see the incredible nature of the Creator.

The Marvel of Sight

Man has never developed a camera lens anywhere near the inconceivable intricacy of the human eye. The human eye is an amazing interrelated system of about forty individual subsystems, including the retina, pupil, iris, cornea, lens, and optic nerve. It has more to it than just the 137 million light-sensitive special cells that send messages to the unbelievably complex brain. About 130 million of these cells look like tiny rods, and they handle the black and white vision. The other seven million are cone shaped and allow us to see in color. The retina cells receive light impressions, which are then translated into electric pulses and sent directly to the brain through the optic nerve.

A special section of the brain called the visual cortex interprets the pulses as color, contrast, depth, etc., which then allows us to see "pictures" of our world. Incredibly, the eye, optic nerve, and visual cortex are totally separate and distinct subsystems. Yet together they capture, deliver, and interpret up to 1.5 million pulse messages per *millisecond!* Think about that for a moment. It would take dozens of computers programmed perfectly and operating together flawlessly to even get close to performing this task.

The eye is an example of what is referred to as "irreducible complexity." It would be absolutely impossible for random processes, operating through gradual mechanisms of genetic mutation and natural selection, to be able to create forty separate subsystems when they provide no advantage to the whole until the very last state of development. Ask yourself how the lens, the retina, the optic nerve, and all the other parts in vertebrates that play a role in seeing not only appeared from nothing, but evolved into interrelated and working parts. Evolutionist Robert Jastrow acknowledges that highly trained scientists could not have improved upon "blind chance":

> The eye appears to have been designed; no designer of telescopes could have done better. How could this marvelous instrument have evolved by chance, through a succession of random events? Many people in Darwin's day agreed with theologian William Pauley, who commented, "There cannot be a design without a designer."[8]

And this marvelous design occurs not just in humans, but in all the different creatures: horses, ants, dogs, whales, lions, flies, ducks, fish, etc. Think about what the theory of evolution claims: the eyes, in working pairs, of all these creatures slowly developed over millions of years. Each of them was blind until all the parts miraculously came together and interrelated with the others, because all parts are needed for the eye to function. Then each creature had its two eyes work in harmony with the brain to interpret those images. Fortunately, each of these creatures simultaneously evolved whatever matching parts each would need: sockets, skin, eyelids, eyelashes, tear ducts, muscles to blink, etc.

You've probably been led to believe that the first simple creatures had rudimentary eyes, and that as creatures slowly evolved their eyes evolved along with them. However, that's not what scientists have found. Not only is there no evidence of this occurring, but some of the most complex eyes have been discovered in the simplest creatures.

Riccardo Levi-Setti, professor emeritus of Physics at the University of Chicago, writes of the trilobite's eye:

> This optical doublet is a device so typically associated with human invention that its discovery in trilobites comes as something of a shock. The realization that trilobites developed and used such devices half a billion years ago makes the shock even greater. And a final discovery—that the refracting interface between the two lens elements in a trilobite's eye was designed in accordance with optical constructions worked out by Descartes and Huygens in the mid-seventeenth century—borders on sheer science fiction ... The design of the trilobite's eye lens could well qualify for a patent disclosure.[9]

How could the amazing seeing eye have come about purely by blind chance? Based on the evidence, wouldn't a reasonable person conclude that the eye is astonishingly complex and could not have evolved gradually, and that each creature's eyes are uniquely designed?

Even Charles Darwin, the father of evolutionary theory, admitted the incredible complexity of the eye in *The Origin of Species:*

> To suppose that the eye, with all its inimitable contrivances for adjusting the focus to different distances, for admitting

different amounts of light, and for the correction of spherical and chromatic aberration, could have formed by natural selection, seems, I freely confess, absurd in the highest degree.[10]

Even more incredible, though, is that Darwin went on to say that he believed the eye could nonetheless have been formed by natural selection. He was right on one point. If a Designer is left out of the equation, such a thought is absurd in the highest degree. And as we will see in detail later, it is contrary to the scientific evidence.

The Wipers

Let's continue with the car analogy. You have windshield wipers which have little squirters. Above the outer corner of each eye are small glands to make tears. Each time you blink, a tiny amount of tear fluid automatically comes out of an opening in your eyelid. It helps wash away germs, dust, and other particles that don't belong in your eye. It also keeps your eye from drying out. Then the fluid drains out of your eye by going into the tear duct. This all happens irrespective of your will. Your eyes sometimes make more tear fluid than normal to protect themselves. For example, this may happen if you are poked in the eye, are in a dusty or smoking area, or are chopping onions.

The Air Conditioner

Think of this air conditioner we call a nose. It's just a protrusion on your face, through which you pull in air, right? Wrong. The nose does more than just smell. It helps us to taste things. It is the main gate to the entire respiratory system, your body's process for breathing.

The nose has two holes called nostrils. The nostrils and the nasal passages are separated by a wall called the septum. Deep inside your nose, close to your skull, your septum is made of very thin pieces of bone. Closer to the tip of your nose, the septum is made of cartilage, which is flexible material that's firmer than skin or muscle but not as hard as bone. Behind your nose is a space called the nasal cavity, which connects with the back of the throat. The nasal cavity is separated from the inside of your mouth by the palate (the roof of your mouth). When you inhale air through your nostrils, the air enters the nasal passages and travels into your nasal cavity. The air then passes down the back of your throat into the trachea, on its way to the lungs.

You may not think about it, but your nose is also a two-way street. When you exhale the old air from your lungs, the nose is the main way for the air to leave your body. But your nose is more than a passageway for air. It also warms, moistens, and filters the air before it goes to the lungs.

The inside of your nose is lined with a moist, thin layer of tissue called a mucous membrane. This membrane warms up the air and moistens it. The mucous membrane makes mucus that captures dust, germs, and other small particles that could irritate your lungs. If you look inside your nose, you will also see hairs that can trap large particles, like dirt or pollen. If something does get trapped in there, you automatically sneeze, and those unwelcome particles speed out of your nose at 100mph.

Further back in your nose are even smaller hairs called cilia that are visible only with a microscope. The cilia move back and forth to move the mucus out of the sinuses and the back of the nose. Cilia also line the air passages, where they help move mucus out of the lungs.

The nose allows you to make "scents" of what's going on in the world around you. Just as your eyes give you information by seeing and your ears help you out by hearing, the nose lets you figure out what's happening by smelling. It does this with help from many parts hidden deep inside your nasal cavity and head.

On the roof of the nasal cavity is the olfactory epithelium, which contains special receptors that are sensitive to odor molecules traveling through the air. These receptors are very small—there are at least 10 million of them in your nose. Think about that for a moment.

There are hundreds of different odor receptors, each with the ability to sense certain odor molecules. Research has shown that an odor can stimulate several different kinds of receptors. The brain interprets the combination of receptors to recognize any one of about 10,000 different smells. So if you are an atheist, you have to add the evolution (the accident) of the nose to the pair of eyes in the accidentally formed hole in the skull in each animal species, both male and female.

Then you have to add a tongue to the mix. Most people just think of the tongue when they think about taste. But you couldn't taste anything without some help from the nose. Besides that, the eyes, nose, brain, and tongue all work in conjunction with each other to get the salivation process working and make eating more pleasurable.

The Sound System

The ear is more than the flap you use to catch sound, and the place to store a pencil when you need to use both hands. Think of the curvature of the ear. Its shape is designed to capture sound and feed it into the amazing computer we call the brain.

We tend to take our ears for granted, and therefore may believe that they happened by random chance through an accidental evolutionary process. So let's also have a quick look at those leathery flaps we (and most creatures) have on each side of our head.

The human ear is a marvel of technology. It is so sensitive you can hear the sound of a cat licking her paws. Your ears are in charge of not only collecting sounds, but also processing them and sending sound signals to your brain. And that's not all—they also help you keep your balance. So if you bend over to pick up your licking cat, you won't fall down.

The ear is extremely delicate and is made up of three different sections: the outer ear, the middle ear, and the inner ear. These parts all work together so you can hear and process sounds. The outer ear has been designed to capture sound, and includes the ear canal, where wax is produced. Earwax contains chemicals to fight off infections that could harm the ear canal. It also collects dirt to help keep the ear canal clean.

> *Since we recognize that the car is obviously designed, why would we think that our much more intricately designed bodies just happened by chance?*

After sound waves enter the outer ear, they travel through the ear canal to the middle ear. The middle ear's main job is to take those sound waves and turn them into vibrations that are delivered to the inner ear. To do this, it needs the ear drum, which is a thin piece of skin stretched tight like a drum. The eardrum separates the outer ear from the middle ear and what are called the ossicles. These are the three smallest and most delicate bones in your body. They include the *malleus,* which is attached to the eardrum and means "hammer" in Latin, the *incus* ("anvil"), which is attached to the malleus, and the *stapes* ("stirrup"), the smallest bone in the body, which is attached to the incus.

As sound waves reach the eardrum, they cause it to vibrate, which moves the tiny ossicles—from the hammer to the anvil and then to the stirrup. These bones help sound move along on its journey into the inner ear.

Sound comes into the inner ear as vibrations and enters the cochlea, a small, curled tube in the inner ear. The cochlea is filled with liquid, which is set into motion, like a wave, when the ossicles vibrate.

The cochlea is also lined with tiny cells covered in tiny hairs that are so small you would need a microscope to see them. They may be small, but they're extremely important. When sound reaches the cochlea, the sound vibrations cause the hairs on the cells to move, creating nerve signals that the brain understands as sound. The brain puts it together so that you hear your favorite song on the radio.

Again, ears do more than hear; they also keep you balanced. In the inner ear are three small loops above the cochlea called semicircular canals. Like the cochlea, they are filled with liquid and have thousands of microscopic hairs. When you move your head, the liquid in the semicircular canals also moves. The liquid moves the tiny hairs, which send a nerve message to your brain about the position of your head. In less than a second, your brain sends messages to the right muscles so that you keep your balance.

As you can see, our body works in many ways similar to a car. You would think I was crazy if I insisted that my car had no maker. Since we recognize that the car is obviously designed, why would we think that our much more intricately designed bodies just happened by chance? It requires intelligence to create purposeful design. That's just common sense.

The Marvel of Science

As mentioned earlier, scientists have made a human-looking robot. In June 2007 the Japan Science and Technology Agency unveiled their Child-Robot with Biometric Body, or CB2 for short. The robot was designed to mimic a one- to two-year-old toddler. It was programmed to sense the environment through 200 optical, auditory, and tactile sensors. It can react, making facial expressions complete with blinking. This is possible through its 51 actuators powered by air to assure smooth movements, although it needs human assistance to stand. Still, the world was astounded by the technological achievement.

So to summarize: Brilliant scientists intentionally made a robot using existing material. This was no accident. They copied the design of the human body and created eyes. Unfortunately, the eyes couldn't see as humans can see. It had ears but it couldn't hear as humans hear. It had a mouth and nose but it could neither eat nor breathe. It couldn't even stand up by itself. Because the bones, muscles, and nerves of the human feet are so complex and interrelated with the balance of the ears and the brain, scientists no doubt didn't know where to begin when designing feet that can stand. Yet, the world (and I'm sure many atheists) marveled at the technology ... and so they should. The scientists who made CB2 should be praised and honored.

Seven Wonders of the World

With all the above in mind, do you really believe that the human skull evolved with holes and sockets in the right places, and then by accident came the brain, interconnected to two eyes, two ears, one nose, skin, blood, nerves, mouth, teeth, tongue, salivary glands, and taste buds, connected to a neck and a body with heart, liver, kidneys, lungs, in both male and female with complex, complementary reproductive systems—and that a similar thing happened throughout *all* the animal kingdom? Many who believe this way think they are intellectually above anyone who concludes that creation was intelligently designed.

A teacher once asked her class to write down the seven natural wonders of the world. As she asked for papers to be passed to the front, one student commented, "But there are so many..."

The teacher discovered that the girl had not written down Mount Everest, the Grand Canyon, etc., but instead had written, "The ability to see, the ability to hear, touch, smell, taste, laugh, and love."

> *The irony when it comes to God and His creation is that many of us have eyes, but don't see.*

Each of these "wonders" is far more wonderful than the Grand Canyon, etc. Our problem is that our understanding of the nature of these God-given gifts is so shallow. Ask a man who just lost his eyesight in an accident if medical science can give him back his vision. We can't make an eye. We can't begin to even plan to make anything that's anywhere close to it. The irony when it comes to God and His creation is that many of us have eyes, but don't see.

So, to go back to the subject of creation giving us evidence that there is a Creator—just as I don't need faith to believe in a builder because I have the building in front of me, so I don't need faith to believe in a Creator, because I have this incredible creation in front of me. All I need is eyes that can see and a brain that works.

Where Does Faith Come In?

I know that offering *proof* of the existence of God flies in the face of what most people believe. Even the most respected Bible teachers say that His existence is a matter of faith. But for years I have disagreed publicly. I'm not trying to be facetious, and I don't think I am naive. I have simply pointed to creation as clear scientific (knowledge-producing) evidence for the existence of a Creator. It's merely common sense.

I want you to notice that in making my case I haven't mentioned faith or the Bible. I have seen many atheists immediately change their minds about God's existence, and then listen to the claims of the gospel, by my pointing to a painting as absolute proof for the existence of a painter, and a building as absolute proof there was a builder ("Every house is built by someone, but He who built all things is God," Hebrews 3:4). Romans 1:20 says that creation leaves the world "without excuse" when it comes to the issue of God's existence.

It is obvious from Scripture that faith isn't needed to know that a Creator exists, because "since the creation of the world His invisible attributes *are clearly seen"* and are "understood." So creation leaves us without excuse because through it God's eternal power and divine nature are *seen*. The Bible tells us that faith is "the evidence of things *not seen"* (Hebrews 11:1, emphasis added).

Psalm 19:1–3 confirms that creation declares the glory of our Creator, and gives proof of His existence throughout all the earth. It says that creation itself "shows knowledge." Remember, the definition of "scientific" is "producing knowledge." Again, faith isn't necessary to know intellectually that God exists, because creation shows us that He does.

Here is where faith plays a part. If I want to go beyond mere belief in a builder and have him *do* something for me, *then* I need to have faith in him. The same applies with God. You don't need to have faith to believe that He exists, because you have creation as the evidence. But if you want God to *do* something for you, then you need to have faith (trust) in Him. The Bible tells us that God rewards those who have faith in Him:

> But without faith it is impossible to please Him, for he who comes to God must believe that He is, and that He is a rewarder of those who diligently seek Him. (Hebrews 11:6)

That is the important difference between intellectual *belief* in God's existence and *faith* (trust) in Him.

So, according to the Bible, atheists are without excuse, although for some strange reason, they deny common sense and reject the revealed knowledge of God.

Another issue where faith is essential is evolution—the theory that everything came into existence without a Creator. In the following chapter, we'll look at the scientific evidence for evolution and see if it's based more on fact or on faith.

One argument that atheists make is that people believe in God only because they were taught to do so as children. They think that gullible young minds were filled with "propaganda" so that they grew up believing in something that isn't true. Let's apply that same reasoning to evolutionary theory. Despite what you were taught throughout your school years, let's see if the evidence is there to justify your faith in evolution.

3

IS EVOLUTION SCIENTIFIC?

"I want to know how God created this world. I am not interested in this or that phenomenon, in the spectrum of this or that element. I want to know His thoughts. The rest are details."

—Albert Einstein

The foundation of atheism is a belief in the theory of evolution. If evolution can prove that we got here by purely naturalistic means, then belief in a Creator would be unnecessary. So in their desire to eliminate God, many people readily choose to believe that evolution is true—without first examining the evidence to make sure the facts support it.

I have lost count of the people I have spoken to who, when asked why they believe that evolution is a fact, immediately say, "Science!" They usually have little to add to that statement.

According to Harvard evolutionist Ernst Mayr, "Evolution is so clearly a fact that you need to be committed to something like a belief in the supernatural if you are at all in disagreement with evolution. It *is* a fact and we don't need to prove it anymore."[11]

If you have gone to public schools, I'm sure you have read similar bold claims hundreds of times, and heard scientists ridicule those who dare to even *question* the concept.

But the dilemma for atheists is to back the claim that evolution is a fact. So let's put evolution to the test and ask if it is "scientific." Consider how this secular website addresses the question "Is Evolution Scientific?":

> Can the theory of evolution be tested? Evolution, when addressing common descent, is largely a historical science. This means that it relates to actions that are supposed to have happened in the distant past, and this makes testing the theory complicated because, unless time travel is invented, we cannot directly test the theory. However, this does not mean that the theory is not testable at all. As with other historical investigations, you can make predictions and retrodictions (to utilize present information or ideas to infer or explain a past event or state of affairs...) based on the theory.
>
> *What this means is that we can state that we would expect to find certain things (say, certain types of fossils) when looking at the historical record, and if those things are found, it supports the theory.* Thus, while we cannot perform the kind of direct tests like we can

in physics and chemistry, the general theory of evolution is testable just as other historical theories are testable.[12] (emphasis added)

Since none of us were there at the beginning, and time travel isn't possible, we will have to rely on historical evidence to piece together what happened in the past. If this theory were true, we would expect to find certain things. To prove the fundamental claims of evolution, we should be able to see evidence of the following:

- How the universe began
- How life came from nonlife
- How we got such diversity of life

If there is no God who created us, there should be plenty of evidence to show that all this came about through random chance and natural processes. Let's see if this hypothesis bears out after we examine the evidence.

Let's start at the beginning: the origin of the universe.

The Origin of the Universe

"In the beginning" ... was God, or the universe? Many people refuse to believe in God because they can't fathom how an entity could be eternal. Yet scientists used to teach that the universe itself was eternal—it just always was—and atheists were content to believe that. So if you believe it is possible for *something* to be eternal (such as the universe), to be logically consistent you would also have to admit it's possible that there is an infinite, omnipotent Being who is eternal.

These days, science has proven that the universe had a beginning. To the creationists' claim that the universe was begun by God, atheists naturally ask, "Then who made God?" It's a very logical question. According to the Law of Cause and Effect, every effect must have a cause. In other words, everything that happens has a catalyst; everything that came into being has something that caused it. Things don't just happen by themselves. For example, if you find a mound of dirt with a G.I. Joe poised on top of it in the middle of your living room, would you just shrug your shoulders and conclude that it spontaneously appeared by itself—or would you suspect that perhaps your young son had something to do with it? It's perfectly reasonable to seek a cause for everything that happens.

Since the evidence proves that the universe is *not* eternal, scientists say it began in an event known as the Big Bang. The Big Bang theory claims that "nothing" suddenly became time, space, matter, and energy, forming a vast, complex, orderly universe composed of over 100 billion galaxies and containing an estimated trillion, trillion, trillion, trillion tons of matter. Now scientists have an even greater dilemma: Where did the initial matter come from? How could something come from nowhere, by itself? Second, what caused it to go "bang"? What was the catalyst that sent the particles flying?

Famed cosmologist Andrei Linde, professor of Physics at Stanford University, is honest about the evolutionists' dilemma:

> The first, and main, problem is the very existence of the big bang. One may wonder, what came before? If space-time did not exist then, how could everything appear from nothing? What arose first? The universe or the laws determining its evolution? Explaining this initial singularity—where and when it all began—still remains the most intractable problem of modern cosmology.[13]

Remember, if a Coke can coming into existence by itself is obvious nonsense, why is the Big Bang theory any more "scientific"?

Searching for answers, scientists recently announced that they may have the puzzle pieces to the fundamental mystery of the universe. Using a NASA telescope, they think they've figured out the cosmic question of where we came from. Their conclusion? Space dust. "In the end, everything comes from space dust," according to Ciska Markwick-Kemper of the University of Manchester in England. This isn't just ordinary space dust, but "dust that was belched from dying stars" about 8 billion light-years from here.[14] Dr. Michael Barlow states that "dust particles in space are the building blocks of comets, planets, and life, yet our knowledge of where this dust was made is still incomplete."[15]

The dilemma is, no matter how far away or how long ago scientists estimate the very first dust particle came from, the logical question remains: Then where did *that* dust come from?

It's unavoidable—at some point, you're forced to conclude that there must be an uncaused cause (a "First Cause") that brought everything else into being. This conclusion agrees with logic, reason, and scientific laws. In all of history, there has never been an instance of anything spontaneously appearing out of nowhere. Something being created from nothing is contrary to all known science. Even Charles Darwin admitted that logically the universe could not have created itself:

> The impossibility of conceiving that this grand and wondrous universe, with our conscious selves, arose through chance, seems to me the chief argument for the existence of God ... I am aware that if we admit a first cause, the mind still craves to know whence it came, and how it arose.[16]

Remember, if a Coke can coming into existence by itself is obvious nonsense, why is the Big Bang theory any more "scientific"?

Even more difficult to explain is how our incredibly fine-tuned universe could be so amazingly complex and orderly. Evolutionist Stephen Hawking, considered the best-known scientist since Albert Einstein, acknowledges:

> The universe and the laws of physics seem to have been specifically designed for us. If any one of about 40 physical qualities had more than slightly different values, life as we know it could not exist: Either atoms would not be stable, or they wouldn't combine into molecules, or the stars wouldn't form the heavier elements, or the universe would collapse before life could develop, and so on.[17]

In short, the evolutionary view cannot offer a logical, scientific explanation for either the origin or the complexity of the universe. There are only two choices: Either no one created everything out of nothing, or Someone—an intelligent, omnipotent, eternal First Cause—created everything out of nothing. Which makes more sense?

The Origin of Life

Another hurdle for evolutionists is to explain how life first appeared on earth. The theory of evolution requires that non-living chemicals somehow developed completely by chance into highly complex, living organisms. However, nonliving things coming to life is the stuff of science fiction, not science. Louis Pasteur's famous experiments have proved the Law of

Biogenesis: that "spontaneous generation" is impossible and that life can arise only from other life. Scientists have spent decades trying to create life in the laboratory in carefully controlled experiments, and have repeatedly failed. If highly intelligent scientists using all the latest, most sophisticated equipment available cannot get the simplest building blocks of life to form—even with the code and materials of life available to them—how could molecules possibly assemble themselves into living cells through only mindless, undirected random chance?

The famous astronomer and mathematician Sir Frederick Hoyle calculated the probability of the spontaneous generation of life:

> No matter how large the environment one considers, life cannot have had a random beginning. Troops of monkeys thundering away at random on typewriters could not produce the works of Shakespeare, for the practical reason that the whole observable universe is not large enough to contain the necessary monkey hordes, the necessary typewriters, and certainly not the waste paper baskets required for the deposition of wrong attempts. The same is true for living material.
>
> The likelihood of the spontaneous formation of life from inanimate matter is one to a number with 40,000 noughts after it ... It is big enough to bury Darwin and

the whole theory of evolution. There was no primeval soup, neither on this planet nor on any other, and if the beginnings of life were not random, they must therefore have been the product of purposeful intelligence.[18]

In Darwin's time, it was assumed that "simple" cells were just primitive blobs of protoplasm, so it wasn't too hard for scientists to envision them assembling by random chance. Because cells can't be seen with the naked eye, scientists mistakenly thought that the chemistry of life was simple. But with today's sophisticated microscopes, molecular biology has shown how vastly complex even a "simple" cell actually is.

Molecular biologist Michael Denton, an evolutionist, acknowledges,

> Although the tiniest bacterial cells are incredibly small, weighing less than 10^{12} grams, each is in effect a veritable micro-miniaturized factory containing thousands of exquisitely designed pieces of intricate molecular machinery, made up altogether of one hundred thousand million atoms, far more complicated than any machinery built by man and absolutely without parallel in the non-living world.[19]

Not only is there no evidence of how life could have come into being, but the more scientists search for answers the more they are astounded at the complexity they find—and the more the evidence shows that life could not have arisen purely by chance. The following statement by geochemist Jeffrey Bada, from the San Diego Scripps Institute, points out the evolutionists' ongoing dilemma concerning this question:

> Today as we leave the twentieth century, we still face the biggest unsolved problem that we had when we entered the twentieth century: How did life originate on Earth?[20]

In 2001, PBS aired the TV series "Evolution," in which they put together all the best information they could find to prove the case for evolution. In a *Washington Post* online forum, producer Richard Hutton was asked, "What are some of the larger questions which are still unanswered by evolutionary theory?" He named several items in his response, but the item topping his list is very telling:

> The origin of life. There is no consensus at all here—lots of theories, little science. That's one of the reasons we didn't cover it in the series. The evidence wasn't very good.[21]

I appreciate his honest admission that all they have is theories—no scientific proof. Don't you think if they had *any* evidence at all, they would have presented it? Could it be that there is no evidence that life arose by natural causes—because life has a Supernatural Cause?

The DNA Factor

Think for a moment if you could ever believe that the book you are holding happened by accident. Here's the argument: There was nothing. Then paper appeared, and ink fell from nowhere onto the flat paper and shaped itself into perfectly formed letters of the English alphabet. Initially, the letters said something like this: "fgsn&k cnlclxc dumbh cckvkduh vstupidm ncncx." As you can see, random letters rarely produce words that make sense. But in time, mindless chance formed them into the order of meaningful words with spaces between them. Periods, commas, capitals, italics, quotes, paragraphs, margins, etc., also came into being in the correct placements. The sentences then grouped themselves so that they related to each other, giving them coherence. Page numbers fell in sequence at the right places, and headers, footers, and footnotes appeared from nowhere on the pages, matching the portions of text to which they related. The paper trimmed itself and bound itself into a book. The ink for the cover fell from different directions, being careful not to incorrectly mingle with the other colors, forming itself into the graphics, title, and author name.

There are multiple copies of this book, so the book then developed the ability to replicate itself thousands of times over.

With this thought in mind, notice that in the following description of DNA, it is likened to a book:

> If you think of your genome (all of your chromosomes) as the book that makes you, then the genes are the words that make up the story ... The letters that make up the words are called DNA bases, and there are only four of them: adenine (A), guanine (G), cytosine (C), and thy-mine (T). It's hard to believe that an alphabet with only four letters can make something as wonderful and complex as a person![22]

To liken DNA to a book is a gross understatement. The amount of information in the 3 billion base pairs in the DNA in every human cell is equivalent to that in 1,000 books of encyclopedia size.[23] It would take a person typing 60 words per minute, eight hours a day, around 50 years to type the human genome. And if all the DNA in your body's 100 trillion cells was put end to end, it would reach to the sun (90 million miles away) and back over 600 times.[24]

Aside from the immense volume of information that your DNA contains, consider whether all the intricate, interrelated parts of this "book" could have come together by sheer chance. Physical chemist Charles Thaxton writes:

> The DNA code is quite simple in its basic structure (although enormously complex in its functioning). By now most

people are familiar with the double helix structure of the DNA molecule. It is like a long ladder, twisted into a spiral. Sugar and phosphate molecules form the sides of the ladder. Four bases make up its "rungs." These are adenine, thymine, guanine, and cytosine. These bases act as the "letters" of a genetic alphabet. They combine in various sequences to form words, sentences, and paragraphs. These base sequences are all the instructions needed to guide the functioning of the cell.

The DNA code is a genetic "language" that communicates information to the cell ... The DNA molecule is exquisitely complex, and extremely precise: the "letters" must be in a very exact sequence. If they are out of order, it is like a typing error in a message. The instructions that it gives the cell are garbled. This is what a mutation is.

The discovery of the DNA code gives the argument from design a new twist. Since life is at its core a chemical code, the origin of life is the origin of a code. A code is a very special kind of order. It represents "specified complexity."[25]

Do you think that DNA's amazing structure could have come together by accident? Or does it point to an intelligent Designer? Even the director of the U.S. National Human Genome Research Institute was forced by the evidence to reason that there is a God. Francis Collins, the scientist who led the team that cracked the human genome, believes there is a rational basis for a Creator and that scientific discoveries bring man "closer to God":

> When you have for the first time in front of you this 3.1-billion-letter instruction book that conveys all kinds of information and all kinds of mystery about human-kind, you can't survey that going through page after page without a sense of awe. I can't help but look at those pages and have a vague sense that this is giving me a glimpse of God's mind.[26]

In 2004, the atheist world was shocked when famed British atheist Antony Flew suddenly announced that he believed in the existence of God. For decades he had heralded the cause of atheism. It was the incredible complexity of DNA that opened his eyes:

> In a recent interview, Flew stated, "It now seems to me that the findings of more than fifty years of DNA research have provided materials for a new and enormously powerful argument to design." Flew also renounced naturalistic theories of evolution:

> "It has become inordinately difficult even to begin to think about constructing a naturalistic theory of the evolution of that first reproducing organism."

In Flew's own words, he simply "had to go where the evidence leads." According to Flew, "...it seems to me that the case for an Aristotelian God who has the characteristics of power and also intelligence, is now much stronger than it ever was before."[27]

DNA is an incredibly detailed language, revealing vast amounts of information encoded in each and every living cell—which could not have arisen by accidental, mindless chance. Information requires intelligence and design requires a designer.

Janet Folger, founder of Faith2Action, reasons,
> Oh, but there is a mountain in South Dakota that proves what evolutionists have been saying all along: that if you just have enough time, wind, rain, erosion, and pure chance, you can get a mountain with the faces of four U.S. presidents on it! If we can all admit that the faces of Mt. Rushmore didn't just accidentally appear, how much more complex are the people standing behind the podiums who want to be president? Here's a question I have ... Which is more complex?

a. The faces of Mt. Rushmore
b. a 747
c. your cell phone
d. a worm

If you guessed "worm," you are right. The DNA structures, digestive system, and reproductive system are far more complex than those other things that obviously had a designer. Maybe, just maybe, someone designed that worm, too.[28]

DNA Comparisons

One typical "proof" given for ape-to-man evolution is that chimpanzees and humans have very similar DNA. In previous DNA studies, based on only portions of the chimp genome, scientists announced that humans and chimps were 98–99 percent identical, depending on what was counted. After completing the mapping of the chimp genome in 2005, evolutionists are now hailing the result as "the most dramatic confirmation yet" that chimps and humans have common ancestry. Their overwhelming "proof" is the finding that the genetic difference is 4 percent—which is interesting proof, because it's actually twice the amount that they've been claiming for years.[29]

In addition, even if the difference is only 4 percent of the 3 billion base pairs of DNA in every cell, that represents *120,000,000 entries* in the DNA code that are different! In our DNA instruction book, that's equivalent to about 12 million words—so that seemingly small percentage has a tremendous impact.[30] Men and monkeys also have another fundamental difference: humans have 23 pairs of chromosomes while chimps have 24, so the DNA isn't as similar as you've been led to believe.

> *DNA is an incredibly detailed language, revealing vast amounts of information encoded in each and every living cell.*

More importantly, this claim of evolutionists makes a huge assumption. What is the scientific basis for assuming that similar DNA means a common ancestor? When you see a biplane and a jet—which share common features of wings, body, tires, engine, controls, etc.—do you assume that one must have evolved from the other naturally, without a maker? That's illogical. It's more reasonable to conclude that similar design indicates a common, intelligent designer. An architect typically uses the same building materials for numerous buildings, and a car manufacturer commonly uses the same parts in various models. So if we have a common Designer, we would expect to find that a similar "blueprint" was used in many different creatures.

After all, DNA is the coding for the way our bodies look and operate, so creatures with similar features or body functions (eyes for vision, enzymes for digestion, etc.) would have similar coding for these things in their DNA. Because human cells have the same biochemical functions as many different animals and even plants, we share some of the same genes. The more we have in common, the more we find similar coding in the blueprints. This is just simple reasoning—not evidence of common ancestry!

So, even though we share 96 percent of our genetic makeup with chimps, that does not mean we are 96 percent chimp. Be careful you don't fall for the illogic of this "evolutionary proof," or scientists will not only make a monkey out of you, they'll make a banana out of you! According to evolutionist Steven Jones, a renowned British geneticist,

> We also share about 50% of our DNA with bananas and that doesn't make us half bananas...[31]

So far, science hasn't provided us with any evidence showing how either the universe or life began. Let's look at our third point—the diversity of life—and see if it fares any better.

4

THE ORIGIN OF SPECIES

"We are intelligent beings, and intelligent beings could not have been formed by a blind, brute, insensible thing..."

—Voltaire

When Darwin wrote *On the Origin of Species*, he had a lot of ideas and conjecture on how this immense variety of life came about. But what evidence do we now have that his ideas were correct?

If evolution were true, and humans and chimps did have a common ancestor, we would expect to find something that *is* half-monkey/half-man. These intermediate stages where one species supposedly evolves into another species are called "transitional forms."

Because evolution is said to have happened in the past, we have to look to paleontology, the science of the study of fossils, to find evidence on the history of life. Well-known French paleontologist Pierre-Paul Grassé explains:

> Naturalists must remember that the process of evolution is revealed only through fossil forms ... Only paleontology

can provide them with the evidence of evolution and reveal its course or mechanisms.[32]

Whether the theory of evolution is a fable or a fact rests on the fossil evidence. If evolution were true, the fossil record should reveal *millions* of transitional forms, as life gradually evolved from one species to another. Darwin understood that evolutionary theory was dependent on these "missing links." He wrote in *Origin of Species:*

> Why, if species have descended from other species by fine gradations, do we not everywhere see innumerable transitional forms? Why is not all nature in confusion, instead of the species being, as we see them, well defined? ... As by this theory innumerable transitional forms must have existed, why do we not find them embedded in countless numbers in the crust of the earth?[33]

Darwin acknowledged that the absence of intermediates put his theory in doubt, but he attributed their lack to the scarcity of fossils at that time—and he had faith that they would eventually be found. However, nearly 150 years later, still nothing has shown up. After scientists have searched diligently *for a century and a half* for evidence, we now have over 100 million fossils catalogued in the world's museums, with 250,000 different species. Surely this should be enough to give us an accurate picture of our past. Remember, paleontology holds the key to whether this theory is true. So do we see the gradual progression from simple life forms to more complex? Did we find the millions of transitional forms that would be expected if evolution were true?

Excited evolutionists believed that they found one back in 1999. A Chinese farmer glued together the head and body of a primitive bird and the tail and hind limbs of a dromaeosaur dinosaur, and completely fooled the worldwide scientific community (including *National Geographic* magazine) into thinking that they had found the "missing link" between carnivorous dinosaurs and modern birds.[34] Called *Archaeoraptor*, it was quickly exposed as a fraud.

Storrs L. Olson, Curator of Birds at the National Muse um of Natural History at the Smithsonian Institution, stated that the feathered dinosaur that was pictured is "simply imaginary and has no place outside of science fiction." He criticized the magazine for publicizing this forgery, saying, "*National Geographic* has reached an all-time low for engaging in sensationalistic, unsubstantiated, tabloid journalism," and he added, "The idea of feathered dinosaurs ... is now fast becoming one of the grander scientific hoaxes of our age."[35]

> *"The idea of feathered dinosaurs ... is now fast becoming one of the grander scientific hoaxes of our age."*

Aside from "feathered dinosaurs," many other supposed "missing links" have been debunked. For example, a Berkeley website claims that "there are numerous examples of transitional forms in the fossil record, providing an abundance of evidence for change over time." The only example they cite as proof is *Pakicetus*. The web site, labeled "Understanding Evolution for Teachers," describes *Pakicetus* as an early ancestor to modern whales. How can scientists tell this? According to the website, "Although pakicetids were land mammals, it is clear that they are related to whales and dolphins based on a number of specializations of the ear, relating to hearing."[36]

In the accompanying illustration, paleontologist Phil Gingerich shows a swimming creature with its forelimbs on the way to becoming flippers, claiming that it is "perfectly intermediate, a missing link between earlier land mammals and later, full-fledged whales."

Although the body he drew does look like a very convincing transitional form, his conclusion was based on only a few fragments of a *skull*. Not a single bone of the body had been found! Once a more complete skeleton was discovered, it proved that *Pakicetus* looked nothing like the creature he imagined.[37]

Besides, many of God's creatures have similar hearing (how many different ways can you make an ear that hears sound?). The eyes of many of God's creatures are very similar. Pigs have skin that is incredibly close to human skin—closer than primates. We both have noses, ears, eyes, liver, kidneys, lungs, teeth, and a brain. Did man evolve from the pig? It would seem so if we are going to be consistent. The pig and man have many features in common.

The creatures Gingerich was looking at were simply different animals with similar hearing ability, created by the same Creator, and his conclusion was nothing but wild and unscientific speculation. Sadly, this happens all too frequently in the evolutionary world. Many alleged "missing links" are based on only a single fossil fragment and the wishful thinking of evolutionists.

After acknowledging that "imaginations certainly took flight over *Archaeoraptor*," a *U.S. News & World Report* writer added:

> *Archaeoraptor* is hardly the first "missing link" to snap under scrutiny. In 1912, fossil remains of an ancient hominid were found in England's Piltdown quarries and quickly dubbed man's apelike ancestor. It took decades to reveal the hoax.[38]

As far as man's supposed ancestry is concerned, the Piltdown Man fraud wasn't an isolated incident. The famed Nebraska Man was derived from a single tooth, which was later found to be from an extinct pig. Java Man, found in the early 20th century, was nothing more than a piece of skull, a fragment of a thigh bone, and three molar teeth. The rest came from the deeply fertile imaginations of plaster of Paris workers. Java Man is now regarded as fully human. Heidelberg Man came from a jawbone, a large chin section, and a few teeth. Most scientists reject the jawbone because it's similar to that of modern man. And don't look to Neanderthal Man for any evidence of evolution. He died of exposure. His skull was exposed as being fully human, not ape. Not only was his stooped posture found to be caused by disease, but he also spoke and was artistic and religious.

In a PBS documentary, Richard Leakey, the world's foremost paleoanthropologist, admitted:

> If pressed about man's ancestry, I would have to unequivocally say that all we have is a huge question mark. To date, there has been nothing found to truthfully purport as a transitional species to man, including Lucy ... If further pressed, I would have to state that there is more evidence to suggest an *abrupt arrival of man rather than a gradual process of evolving.*[39] (emphasis added)

Even the classic example of horse evolution is fictionalized. Evolutionist Boyce Rensberger addressed a symposium attended by 150 scientists at the Field Museum of Natural History in Chicago, which considered problems facing the theory of evolution. He describes what the fossil evidence reveals for horses:

> The popularly told example of horse evolution, suggesting a gradual sequence of changes from four-toed, fox-sized creatures, living nearly 50 million years ago, to today's

much larger one-toed horse, has long been known to be wrong. Instead of gradual change, fossils of each intermediate species *appear fully distinct, persist unchanged,* and then become extinct. Transitional forms are unknown.[40] (emphasis added)

This is the case not just for horses, but throughout the entire animal kingdom. Rather than the millions of transitional forms evolutionists would expect to find, all we have at best are a handful of disputable examples. Harvard paleontologist Stephen Jay Gould writes,

The extreme rarity of transitional forms in the fossil record persists as the trade secret of paleontology. The evolutionary trees that adorn our textbooks have data only at the tips and nodes of their branches; the rest is inference, however reasonable, not the evidence of fossils ... All paleontologists know that the fossil record contains precious little in the way of intermediate forms; transitions between major groups are characteristically abrupt.[41]

This brings us to a very interesting point...

Cambrian Explosion

As pointed out above, rather than transitional forms between species, what the fossil record reveals is that each species appears fully distinct and remains unchanged. Despite what you've been taught in school, the fossil evidence does *not* show that all life evolved from a single common ancestor through minor changes.

Instead, during the period that paleontologists call the Cambrian Explosion, virtually all the major animal forms appear suddenly without any trace of less complex ancestors. No new body plans have come into existence since then. The Cambrian Explosion is also known as "The Biological Big Bang," because the majority of complex life forms show up virtually overnight. If the entire period of life on earth was a 24-hour day, the Cambrian period would be less than two minutes. Like the Big Bang that supposedly began our universe, out of nowhere, nothing suddenly became everything.

T.S. Kemp, curator of the zoological collections at the Oxford University Museum of Natural History, is one of the world's foremost experts on Cambrian fossils. In discussing the sudden appearance of new species, Kemp writes,

> With few exceptions, radically new kinds of organisms appear for the first time in the fossil record already fully evolved, with most of their characteristic features present ... It is not at all what might have been expected.[42]

Nature clearly does not reveal the continuous picture that evolution requires. Instead, life forms are strictly separated into very distinct categories. Paleontologist Robert Carroll, an evolutionist authority, admits this fact in his book *Pat terns and Processes of Vertebrate Evolution:*

> Although an almost incomprehensible number of species inhabit Earth today, they do not form a continuous spectrum of barely distinguishable intermediates. Instead, nearly all species can be recognized as belonging to a relatively limited number of clearly distinct major groups, with very few illustrating intermediate structures or ways of life.[43]

So according to the evidence produced by paleontology—our guide to whether or not evolution is true—life did *not* evolve gradually over a long period from simple to complex forms. Instead, the fossils show that all the major animals groups appeared fully formed, all at one time. This isn't what evolutionists expected, but it is exactly what we would expect to find if *creation* were true: each organism is fully developed, genetically separated into kinds, and change is limited.

Regarding the Cambrian fauna, prominent British evolutionist Richard Dawkins made the following observation:

> And we find many of them already in an advanced state of evolution, the very first time they appear. It is as though they were just planted there, without any evolutionary history. Needless to say, this appearance of sudden planting has delighted creationists...[44]

Naturally, Dawkins surmises why there may be a lack of any intermediates and attributes the "very important gaps" to "imperfections in the fossil record." He then adds, "If you are a creationist you may think that this is special pleading"—and he's correct. He goes on to say:

> Both schools of [evolutionary] thought agree that the only alternative explanation of the sudden appearance of so many complex animal types in the Cambrian era is divine creation, and both would reject this alternative.[45]

Dawkins was right. As a creationist I *am* delighted that the scientific evidence so consistently reveals the truth about the origins of this incredible creation. But I would be delighted beyond words if atheists would overcome their bias against the truth and acknowledge its unspeakably incredible Creator.

5
MUTANT TURTLES

"Who are you going to believe, me or your own two eyes?"

—Groucho Marx

The story is told of a symbolic foot race that took place between Russia and the U.S. during the Cold War. The very best athlete from each country competed to see who was superior. The American runner won. The next day, the Soviet newspaper headline read: "Russia comes in second in big race; U.S. comes in next to last."

As this humorous story shows, your perspective makes all the difference. The way you present the evidence has a great impact on the way it is perceived—but it doesn't affect reality. So with that in mind, let's take a close look at an article in the *Encyclopedia Britannica* describing the turtle's evolution:

> The evolution of the turtle is one of the most remarkable in the history of vertebrates. Unfortunately, the origin of this highly successful order is obscured by the *lack of fossils,* although turtles leave *more*

and better fossil remains than do other vertebrates. By the middle of the Triassic Period (about 200,000,000 years ago) turtles were numerous and in possession of basic turtle characteristics ... *Intermediates* between turtles and cotylosaurs, the primitive reptiles from which turtles probably sprang, *are entirely lacking.*[46] (emphasis added)

At first glance, this could certainly give the perception that turtles are a marvelous example of evolution. But read it again—and think about what you read. Rather than the exciting, clear-cut proof of evolution that it claims to be, here is what it's really saying:

- Due to the lack of fossils, there is no clue to the turtle's origin.
- When it first appeared, the turtle looked just like a turtle.
- Despite leaving more fossils, and better fossils, than other vertebrates, there are *no* intermediate forms.
- Its structure hasn't changed since it appeared.

So the turtle arrived on the scene fully formed, there are no fossils linking it to any other creature, and it's remaining as a turtle. Sounds like evidence that would delight any creationist. Yet supposedly we've just seen "one of the *most remarkable*" examples of evolution! Your perspective makes all the difference. So what do *you* see? Do you see a creature that gradually evolved from less complex life forms, linked to its ancestors by numerous transitional forms? Or do you see a creature that was created in its own distinct kind, and is consistently reproducing after its own kind?

Also, with "more and better fossil remains" for the turtle than other vertebrates, but transitional forms still "entirely lacking," what does this say about the intermediates between all other vertebrates? I think the encyclopedia is right about one thing: It *is* "one of the most remarkable" examples of evolution available—since no such evidence exists, the "nothing" they've found so far is the best there is.

As we've seen previously, there is no fossil evidence that evolution actually took place. But aside from that minor detail, let's explore how scientists propose that evolution occurs. The theory of evolution claims that all the amazing complexity we see throughout creation comes about through undirected processes by means of mutations and natural selection. So, in essence, there are "mutant turtles"! Turtles, and all living things, have allegedly evolved from other creatures through a series of random mutations. Theoretically, if a mutation ("copying error") occurs in the genes, and happens to give the creature some benefit, then this benefit is passed on to offspring through the process of natural selection.

If this is truly possible, we shouldn't have any problem seeing plenty of evidence of this taking place.

Microevolution vs. Macroevolution

It's important to realize that there is such a thing as *micro-evolution*—that is, variation within species. Look at the variety within dogs—the tiny Chihuahua to the huge Great Dane. Both are dogs and they have incredible differences. But they are still dogs. Or look at horses. Within the horse family are the donkey, zebra, draft horse, and the dwarf pony. All are different, but all are horses. There are huge variations within the human species. Think of all the different features from Asian to African to Aboriginal to Caucasian. But we are all within the same species, *Homo sapiens*.

Darwin's theory of evolution, however, is based on the concept of *macro*evolution. This is the inference that successive small changes seen in *micro* evolution (these variations within species) can accumulate and lead to large changes over long periods of time. In macroevolution, one kind of creature (such as a reptile) becomes another kind of creature (such as a bird), requiring the creation of entirely new features and body types. This would be a bit like observing a car going from 0 to 60mph in 60 seconds, and inferring that it can then go 0 to 6,000mph in 100 minutes—and become an airplane in the process.

That's quite an assumption, and it puts a tremendous responsibility on mutations to accidentally create complex new body parts, and on natural selection to recognize the benefit these new parts will eventually convey and make sure the creatures with those new parts survive. As Stephen J. Gould explains,

> The essence of Darwinism lies in a single phrase: natural selection is the creative force of evolutionary change. No one denies that selection will play a negative role in eliminating the unfit. Darwinian theories require that it create the fit as well.[47]

Let's take a closer look at how mutations and natural selection supposedly work to create the amazing complexity of life in our world.

It Doesn't Add Up

The first problem we find is that the variations we see in micro evolution are always within limits set by the genetic code. Fifty years of genetic research on the fruit fly have convinced evolutionists that change is limited and confined to a defined population. Despite being bombarded with mutation agents for half a century, the mutant fruit flies continue to exist as fruit flies, leading geneticists to acknowledge that they will not evolve into something else. This confirms Gregor Mendel's findings in the 1800s that there are natural limits to genetic change.

Genetics professor Francisco Ayala is quoted as saying: "I am now convinced from what the paleontologists say that small changes do not accumulate."[48] Small changes aren't the only thing that doesn't add up. But more importantly, the amount of change isn't really the issue.

Mutations can only modify or eliminate existing structures, not create new ones. Within a particular type of creature, hair can vary from curly to straight, legs can vary from heavy to thin, beaks from long to short, wings from dark to light, etc. But the creatures still have hair, legs, beaks, and wings—nothing new has been added.

> *Creation of new body parts would be equivalent to a "telegram" giving rise to "encyclopedias" of meaningful, useful genetic sentences.*

If you recall, in our DNA book, a mutation is a mistake—a "typing error." In the genetic blueprint, the letters that define these features can occasionally be rearranged or lost through mutations, but none of this will account for the additions needed by macroevolution. Remember, in the molecules-to-man theory, everything evolved from simple cells to complex life forms. So if a fish were to grow legs and lungs, or a reptile were to grow wings, that creature's genetic information would have to increase to create the new body parts. This would be equivalent to a "telegram" giving rise to "encyclopedias" of meaningful, useful genetic sentences.

Think how much more information there is in the human genome than in the bacterial genome. If macroevolution were true, where did all that vastly complex new information come from? *Scientists have yet to find even a single mutation that increases genetic information.* As physicist Lee Spetner puts it, "Information cannot be built up by mutations that lose it. A business can't make money by losing it a little at a time."[49]

Mutating Theory

Many people have been led to believe that organisms often develop favorable mutations based on their environments. For example, it's often thought that bacteria can become resistant to antibiotics, thus proving that they evolve. But the website "Understanding Evolution" (produced by the University of California Museum of Paleontology and the National Center for Science Education), explains how mutations work:

> Mutations do not "try" to supply what the organism "needs." ... For example, exposure to harmful chemicals may increase the mutation rate, but will not cause more mutations that make the organism resistant to those chemicals. In this respect, mutations are random—whether a particular

mutation happens or not is unrelated to how useful that mutation would be.[50]

To illustrate, they explain that where people have access to shampoos with chemicals that kill lice, there are a lot of lice that are resistant to those chemicals. So either: 1) resistant strains of lice were always there—and are just more frequent now because all the non-resistant lice died; or 2) exposure to lice shampoo actually caused mutations that provide resistance to the shampoo. Based on the scientific evidence, they conclude that "the first explanation is the right one and that directed mutations, the second possible explanation relying on non-random mutation, is not correct."[51]

After numerous experiments, researchers have found that none unambiguously support directed mutation. In the case of bacteria, scientific experiments have proved that "the penicillin-resistant bacteria were there in the population before they encountered penicillin. They did not evolve resistance in response to exposure to the antibiotic."

Therefore, mutations are not logical adaptations that make a creature better suited for its environment. They are completely random—the result of mindless, undirected chance.

Even if these random mutations *could* happen to cause a lump of a wing to begin to form, how would that help the creature to survive? In evolutionary theory, natural selection will enable the survival of creatures that develop some sort of benefit. But until it becomes a fully formed wing, any stub would be more of a detriment than a benefit. Consider the following observations from noted evolutionists:

> The reasons for rejecting Darwin's proposal were many, but first of all that many innovations cannot possibly come into existence through accumulation of many small steps, and even if they can, natural selection cannot accomplish it, because incipient and intermediate stages are not advantageous.[52]
> —Embryologist Soren Lovtrup

> But how do you get from nothing to such an elaborate something if evolution must proceed through a long sequence of intermediate stages, each favored by natural selection? You can't fly with 2% of a wing...[53]
> —Paleontologist Stephen Jay Gould

> Darwinism is claiming that all the adaptive structures in nature, all the organisms which have existed throughout history were generated by the accumulation of entirely undirected mutations. That is an *entirely unsubstantiated belief* for which there is not the slightest evidence whatsoever.[54] (emphasis added)

—Molecular biologist Michael Denton

Mutations do *not* work as a mechanism to fuel the evolutionary process. They are random instead of purposeful, and they only modify or remove information, but never add it—a requirement of the theory. Any mutation that supposedly creates a transitional form would be far more likely to doom the poor creature than to help it up the evolutionary chain. But don't just take my word for it. About 150 of the world's leading evolutionary theorists gathered at a Macro evolution Conference in Chicago to consider the question, "Are mutation and natural selection enough?" Evolutionist Roger Lewin sums up the conclusion of the conference:

> The central question of the Chicago conference was whether the mechanisms underlying *micro* evolution can be extrapolated to explain the phenomena of *macro*evolution. At the risk of doing violence to the positions of some of the people at the meeting, the answer can be given as a clear, *No.*[55]

Please thoughtfully read this response from evolutionist Michael Denton, author of *Evolution: A Theory in Crisis*. Asked in an interview if Darwinian theory adequately explained what we see in nature, he very honestly admitted its weaknesses:

The basic pattern it fails to explain is the apparent uniqueness and isolation of major types of organisms ... It strikes me as being a flagrant denial of common sense to swallow that all these things were built up by accumulative small random changes. This is simply a nonsensical claim, especially for the great majority of cases, where nobody can think of any credible explanation of how it came about. And this is a very profound question which everybody skirts, everybody brushes over, everybody tries to sweep under the carpet.

The fact is that the majority of these complex adaptations in nature cannot be adequately explained by a series of intermediate forms. And this is a fundamental problem. Common sense tells me there must be something wrong.[56]

Evolutionary theory is a "nonsensical claim" that is a "flagrant denial of common sense," yet this is the story that we're told repeatedly is a proven fact. There *is* something wrong.

> *Mutations are random instead of purposeful, and they only modify or remove information, but never add it—a requirement of the theory.*

The truth is that mutations cannot create any new features, or new creatures, which explains why the transitional forms that evolution requires just aren't there. To skirt around the fact that the evidence refutes Darwin's theory of gradualism, some scientists have proposed their own theory: *punctuated equilibrium*. This theory, championed by Stephen Gould and others, proposes that evolution happened in rapid spurts (by some mysterious genetic mechanism) followed by long periods of stability. They suggest that species had to evolve quickly based on sudden changes in their environment, such as a flood or drought.

There are a couple of problems with this theory as well. First, according to the website "Understanding Evolution," which explains evolution to teachers, "Factors in the environment ... are not generally thought to influence the direction of mutation." They state that experiments showed mutations "did not occur because the organism was placed in a situation where the mutation would be useful."[57] Again, mutations are completely random and *not* based on the environment. So if there's no evidence to show that mutations could cause creatures to evolve gradually over millions of years, why would we think they could somehow manage to evolve very rapidly?

Second, there is nothing in the fossil record that would lead us to believe this was the case. Very conveniently for proponents of this theory, evolution supposedly occurred so quickly that there wasn't time to leave any fossils as evidence. The theory of punctuated equilibrium was proposed only as a way to explain the *lack* of fossil evidence. I'm afraid the only thing actually evolving is their theory.

In his book *Darwinism: The Refutation of a Myth,* Swedish embryologist Soren Lovtrup writes, "I suppose that nobody will deny that it is a great misfortune if an entire branch of science becomes addicted to a false theory. But this is what has happened in biology ... I believe that one day the Darwinian myth will be ranked the greatest deceit in the history of science."[58] I hope you won't continue to fall for it.

Leftovers Again?

There's one last point I'd like to bring up about evolution. Most likely you've heard that "vestigial organs" are proof that we've evolved from more primitive forms. Because these organs supposedly have no purpose, evolutionists assume they have outlived their usefulness and are "leftovers" from our less advanced ancestors.

But even if an organ were no longer needed, wouldn't it only prove *devolution?* This fits well with the Law of Entropy—all things deteriorate over time. What evolution requires, however, is not the loss but the *addition* of information, where an organism *increases* in complexity. So "vestigial organs" still wouldn't help the evolutionist's case.

Besides, it's not even scientifically possible to prove that something has no use, because its use can always be discovered as more information becomes available. And that's exactly what has happened. It was claimed at the Scopes trial that there are "no less than 180 vestigial structures in the human body, sufficient to make of a man a veritable walking museum of antiquities."[59] Today the list has shrunk to virtually zero. Scientists have now discovered that each of these organs does indeed have a purpose: for example, the appendix is part of the human immune system, and the "tailbone" actually supports muscles that are necessary for daily bodily functions.

In their zeal to provide evidence of evolution, scientists have proclaimed organs as useless simply because they were ignorant of their functions at the time. They were there all along, but evolutionists just didn't know it.

Isn't it possible that the same could be true for God's existence? You may be ignorant of His presence at the time, but that doesn't mean He doesn't exist. If you look, you will find that He was there all along. You can *know* that God exists.

6
SCIENCE AND ATHEISM

"A little science estranges men from God, but much science leads them back to Him."

—Louis Pasteur

Many atheists are tolerant people, respectful of the religious beliefs of others. Some, however, are offended by the very thought of faith. Consider the attitude of Richard Dawkins, arguably the world's most famous atheist:

> It is fashionable to wax apocalyptic about the threat to humanity posed by the AIDS virus, "mad cow" disease, and many others, but I think a case can be made that faith is one of the world's great evils, comparable to the smallpox virus but harder to eradicate.[60]

It isn't *faith* that is the problem. We all have faith in something. Many place their faith in God; atheists place their faith in man—and especially in evolution, which supposedly eradicates God. According to philosopher Malcolm Muggeridge, to those whose faith is in the "religion of evolution," any "nonbelievers" are considered unenlightened:

> The dogmatism of science has become a new orthodoxy, disseminated by the Media and a State educational system with thoroughness and subtlety far exceeding anything of the kind achieved by the Inquisition; to the point that to believe today in a miraculous happening like the Virgin birth is to appear a kind of imbecile, whereas to disbelieve in an unproven and unprovable scientific proposition like the Theory of Evolution, and still more to question some quasi-scientific shibboleth like the Population Explosion, is to stand condemned as an obscurantist, an enemy of progress and enlightenment.[61]

Some prominent atheists are hard at work today to convince the public that refusing to believe in evolution makes one an uneducated, backwards, flat-earth ignoramus. What's ironic is that agnostics—those who don't *know* if God exists ("those who profess ignorance")—are labeling as "ignorant" those who *do* know God. Dawkins, renowned evolutionary biologist from Oxford and author of *The God Delusion*, writes:

> In childhood our credulity serves us well. It helps us to pack, with extraordinary rapidity, our skulls full of the wisdom of our parents and our ancestors. But if we don't grow out of it in the fullness of time, our ... nature makes us a sitting target for astrologers, mediums, gurus, evangelists, and quacks. We need to replace the automatic

credulity of childhood with the constructive skepticism of adult science[62] ... You cannot be both sane and well educated and disbelieve in evolution. The evidence is so strong that any sane, educated person has got to believe in evolution[63] ... It is absolutely safe to say that, if you meet somebody who claims not to believe in evolution, that person is ignorant, stupid or insane (or wicked, but I'd rather not consider that).[64]

It seems that Mr. Dawkins is ignorant of how many "ignorant," "stupid," "insane," and "wicked" people believe in a Creator. Most of the great scientists of the past who founded and developed the key disciplines of science were creationists. Note the following sampling:
- Physics: Newton, Faraday, Maxwell, Kelvin
- Chemistry: Boyle, Dalton, Pascal, Ramsay
- Biology: Ray, Linnaeus, Mendel, Pasteur
- Geology: Steno, Woodward, Brewster, Agassiz
- Astronomy: Kepler, Galileo, Herschel, Maunder[65]

> As this list of great scientists attests, those who believe in a Creator are far from "anti-science" or anti-intellectual.

Dawkins also promotes the idea that religion "subverts science and saps the intellect." But as this list of great scientists attests, those who believe in a Creator are far from "antiscience" or anti-intellectual. In fact, these are some of the greatest minds in the history of science—the people who actually made most of the discoveries that created modern science to begin with. For example, Isaac Newton, arguably the most influential scientist in history, managed to discover the composition of light, deduce the laws of motion, invent calculus, compute the speed of sound, and define universal gravitation—all while believing that our universe "could only proceed from the counsel and dominion of an intelligent and powerful Being."

Although evolutionists often claim that science and religion are incompatible, the reality is that modern science was born of a belief in an unchanging God of order, purpose, and consistency. Consider the following statements from some of the world's most eminent scientists:

> Science is the glimpse of God's purpose in nature. The very existence of the amazing world of the atom and radiation points to a purposeful creation, to the idea that there is a God and an intelligent purpose back of everything ... An orderly universe testifies to the greatest statement ever uttered: "In the beginning, God..."

—Arthur H. Compton, Nobel Prize winner in Physics

The chief aim of all investigation of the external world should be to discover the rational order and harmony which has been imposed on it by God.
—Johann Kepler

With regard to the origin of life, science ... positively affirms creative power.
—Lord Kelvin

All material things seem to have been composed of the hard and solid particles abovementioned, variously associated in the first creation by the counsel of an intelligent Agent. For it became Him who created them to set them in order. And if He did so, it's unphilosophical to seek for any other origin of the world, *or to pretend that it might arise out of a chaos by the mere laws of nature.* (emphasis added)
—Sir Isaac Newton

The more I study nature, the more I stand amazed at the work of the Creator.
—Louis Pasteur

There is not a shred of objective evidence to support the hypothesis that life began in an organic soup here on the earth ... So why do biologists indulge in unsubstantiated fantasies in order to deny what is so patently obvious, that the 200,000 amino acid chains, and hence life, did not appear by chance?

—Frederick Hoyle

These men are not the only scientists who weren't persuaded to become believers in the theory of evolution. Michael Ruse, a preeminent evolutionist, wrote in *New Scientist:*

> An increasing number of scientists, most particularly a growing number of evolutionists ... argue that Darwinian evolutionary theory is no genuine scientific theory at all ... Many of the critics have the highest intellectual credentials.[66]

Jerry Bergman, Ph.D., has compiled a list of almost 3,000 scientists and professors who reject evolution, most of whom hold Ph.D.s in science. He believes that, given the time and resources, he could easily complete a list of 10,000 names.[67] In fact, according to Dr. Francis Collins, director of the Human Genome Project, 40 percent of working scientists claim to be believers. As a believer himself, Collins finds exploring nature to be "a way of getting a glimpse of God's mind," and observes, "All truth is God's truth, and therefore God can hardly be threatened by scientific discoveries."[68]

Isaac Newton believed that religious inquiry and scientific investigation complemented each other. He felt there were truths to be found in both of the "books" authored by God—the Book of Scripture and the Book of Nature. Francis Bacon, founder of the scientific method, called them the "book of God's word" and the "book of God's works." Both of these books provide abundant evidence for a Creator.

Maybe that's why, despite decades of evolutionary teaching to indoctrinate young minds, nearly 8 in 10 Americans still are not buying the theory. (In a 2007 Newsweek poll, 48 percent said God created humans in the present form at one time in the last 10,000 years or so, another 30 percent believe God guided the process—so 78 percent attribute creation to God. Only 13 percent believe in naturalistic evolution.[69]) They've heard all the arguments and the claims of evidence, but they apparently lack the faith to be true believers in the theory. Evolution just doesn't add up.

Happy Coincidence

Look at how awkwardly physicist Freeman J. Dyson of Princeton's Institute for Advanced Study tries to explain the design of the universe:

> As we look out into the universe and identify *the many accidents* of physics and astronomy that have worked to our benefit, it almost seems as if the universe must in some sense have known that we were coming.[70] (empha sis added)

Physicist and Nobel laureate Arno Penzias, in contemplating this amazing design in our universe, came to a similar conclusion:

> Astronomy leads us to a unique event, a universe that was created out of nothing and delicately balanced to provide exactly the conditions required to support life. In the absence of an *absurdly improbable accident,* the observations of modern science seem to suggest an underlying, one might say, supernatural plan.[71] (emphasis added)

Speaking of the absurdly improbable, Harvard biologist Stephen Jay Gould described humans as "a glorious accident" of evolution which required *60 trillion contingent events.* With cosmologists estimating the Earth to be 4.55 billion years old, to accomplish those 60 trillion events would require more than 36 necessary events per day, each day for 4.55 billion years—just to get *Homo sapiens.* And conveniently, each of these 36 daily new events just happened to occur in the right place at the right time in the right sequence. And this doesn't take into account the astronomical number of "accidents" necessary to form the tens, perhaps hundreds of thousands of separate ecosystems.

One individual put it this way: The odds would be better of getting hit by lightning at the moment you won the Powerball lottery while dying in the crash of a plane that got struck by a meteor. But then, such things don't happen every day.

Way back in 1950, in his book *The Nature of the Universe*, astronomer Sir Fred Hoyle also argued for accidental coincidence to explain the many unique but necessary properties of the universe and of our own planet. But the discoveries of the following thirty years dramatically changed his mind, as described in his book *The Intelligent Universe*. In 1983 he said,

> Such properties seem to run through the fabric of the natural world like a thread of *happy coincidences*. But there are *so many odd coincidences* essential to life that some explanation seems required to account for them.[72]

It is easy to understand why many scientists like Hoyle have changed their minds in recent years. It doesn't take a rocket scientist to figure out that this amazing universe can't be explained as a series of happy coincidental accidents that were the result of a thinking universe that knew we were coming. This is why Frederic B. Burnham, a well-known historian of science, declared, "The scientific community is prepared to consider the idea that God created the universe a more respectable hypothesis today than at any time in the last 100 years."[73]

Faith in Science

Many times people reject faith in God simply because they put their faith in science. However, *science* (not religion) once thought that the Earth was flat, that it sat on a foundation of large animals, and that the sun rose and set. It thought that the Earth was the center of the solar system. It didn't know that the surface of the Earth was spinning at over 1,000 miles per hour, that the continents move, and that bowling balls don't fall faster than marbles. Among a multitude of incorrect ideas, it once believed that there were nine planets in our solar system and that heavier-than-air objects can't have sustained flight unless they can flap their wings.

Science is forever changing its mind. Many things science believes today will be laughed at in one hundred years. I'm sure you've been led to believe that science provides us with facts and proofs that we can place our trust in. But the field of science actually cannot give us any *knowledge* at all. Despite the fact that the very meaning of the word "science" is "knowledge," science can never truly *know* anything, as Bertrand Russell explains:

> A religious creed differs from a scientific theory in claiming to embody eternal and absolutely certain truth, whereas science is always tentative, expecting that modification in its present theories will sooner or later be found necessary, and aware that its method is one which is logically incapable of arriving at a complete and final demonstration.[74]

Richard Phillips Feynman, an accomplished American physicist, stated, "If you thought that science was certain— well, that is just an error on your part."[75] Since all scientific statements are open to reevaluation as new data is acquired, the reality is that science can never establish anything as "truth" or "fact." No scientific statement is ever formally beyond question. So whenever "proof" is mentioned in a scientific context, it is inaccurate.[76]

Why then would evolutionists like Ernst Mayr falsely claim that evolution "is a fact and we don't need to prove it anymore"? Perhaps they try to convince people that evolution has already been conclusively proven ... because they have no actual proof to offer. There is no concrete evidence for the theory of evolution. *There isn't any.* It's simply an idea that cannot be backed up with evidence. How then can anyone think that the theory of evolution is scientific?

Information theorist Hubert Yockey rightly observed:

> One must conclude that, contrary to the established and current wisdom, a scenario describing the genesis of life on earth by chance and natural causes which can be accepted on the basis of *fact* and *not faith* has not yet been written.[77] (emphasis added)

Many years ago I saw a cartoon showing two men in lab coats standing at a blackboard, with an elaborate, complex equation filling the board. In the middle of the equation was written: "Then a miracle occurs." I remember that cartoon every time I think of the theory of evolution. There are so many miracles that must occur for evolution to be true that I'm amazed at the great faith shown by those who believe in it. In fact, it seems to me that atheists are the most faith-filled people on earth.

Remember the conditions mentioned in Chapter 3 to test evolution scientifically: *"We can state that we would expect to find certain things (say, certain types of fossils) when looking at the historical record, and if those things are found, it supports the theory."* To determine if the theory is true, let's recap the scientific evidence for evolution and see if it supports the theory. We'll add a corroborating statement from the atheist's authority—evolutionary scientists:

- **Origin of the universe:** We've seen that it cannot have come into existence by itself—something cannot come from nothing. To do so would contradict known scientific laws. According to the First Law of Thermodynamics (the law of conservation of energy), matter and energy can be neither created nor destroyed.

  [The Big Bang] represents the instantaneous suspension of physical laws, the sudden, abrupt flash of lawlessness that allowed something to come out of nothing. It represents a true *miracle*—transcending physical principles.[78]
  —Physicist Paul Davies

- **Origin of life:** We've seen that it cannot have come into existence by itself—life cannot come from nonlife. To do so would contradict known scientific laws. According to the Law of Biogenesis, life arises only from preexisting life.

    The complexity of the simplest known type of cell is so great that it is impossible to accept that such an object could have been thrown together suddenly by some kind of freakish, vastly improbable, event. Such an occurrence would be indistinguishable from a *miracle*.[79]
    —Molecular biologist Michael Denton

- **Origin of species:** We've seen that the incredible diversity of life cannot arise from a simple cell. To do so would contradict known scientific laws. According to the Law of Biogenesis, life perpetuates itself—kinds only reproduce their own kinds. Also, according to the Second Law of Thermodynamics (the law of increasing entropy), every ordered system over time tends to become more disordered; things do not become more complex.

    There are no detailed Darwinian accounts for the evolution of any fundamental biochemical or cellular system, only a variety of *wishful speculations*. It is

remarkable that Darwinism is accepted as a satisfactory explanation for such a vast subject—evolution—with so little rigorous examination of how well its basic theses work in illuminating specific instances of biological adaptation or diversity.[80]
—Molecular biologist James Shapiro

Evolutionists can make all the bold claims they like, but in the end the best science can offer is: "Then a miracle occurs." Based on the evidence, would a reasonable person conclude that evolution is based more on science, or on faith?

Even Voltaire, often considered an atheist, believed that the existence of a Creator was reasonable. (While his criticisms denounced the actions of organized religion, he participated in religious activities and even erected a chapel on his estate.) He stated, "What is faith? Is it to believe that which is evident? No. It is perfectly evident to my mind that there exists a necessary, eternal, supreme, and intelligent being. This is no matter of faith, but of reason."[81]

Antony Flew, the famous atheist turned deist, explains how his journey to the "discovery of the Divine has been a pilgrimage of reason":

> There were two factors in particular that were decisive. One was my growing empathy with the insight of Einstein and other noted scientists that there had to be

an Intelligence behind the integrated complexity of the physical Universe. The second was my own insight that the integrated complexity of life itself—which is far more complex than the physical Universe—can only be explained in terms of an Intelligent Source. I believe that the origin of life and reproduction simply cannot be explained from a biological standpoint despite numerous efforts to do so.

With every passing year, the more that was discovered about the richness and inherent intelligence of life, the less it seemed likely that a chemical soup could magically generate the genetic code. The difference between life and non-life, it became apparent to me, was ontological and not chemical. The best confirmation of this radical gulf is Richard Dawkins' comical effort to argue in *The God Delusion* that the origin of life can be attributed to a "lucky chance." If that's the best argument you have, then the game is over. No, I did not hear a Voice. It was the evidence itself that led me to this conclusion.[82]

Professor Theodore Roszak sums up the situation:

The irony is devastating. The main purpose of Darwinism was to drive every last trace of an incredible God from biology. But the theory replaces God with an even more incredible deity—omnipotent chance.[83]

In their desire to eliminate God, evolutionists have devised an eternal, omnipotent, life-giving, intelligent designer, and called it Chance. They don't have any proof to *know* that their "creator" exists, they just have a strong faith that it does. Christians, on the other hand, have the evidence to prove that their eternal, omnipotent, life-giving, intelligent Designer exists, and they not only *know* He exists, they *know Him*.

Now let's quickly review the evidence and see if it's better explained by the existence of a Creator—with a corroborating statement from the Christian's authority, God's Word:

- **Origin of the universe:** The universe began in an instant, is expanding, and exhibits design, order, and complexity. Every effect must have a Cause, and design must have a Designer.

    > Thus says God the LORD, who created the heavens and stretched them out, who spread forth the earth and that which comes from it, who gives breath to the people on it, and spirit to those who walk on it. (Isaiah 42:5)

- **Origin of life:** Life cannot arise spontaneously but comes only from preexisting life.

    > Nor is [God] worshiped with men's hands, as though He needed anything, since

He gives to all life, breath, and all things. (Acts 17:25)

- **Origin of species:** Creatures exist in discrete kinds, which appeared fully formed all at once and remain virtually unchanged.

God created great sea creatures and every living thing that moves, with which the waters abounded, according to their kind, and every winged bird according to its kind ... And God made the beast of the earth according to its kind, cattle according to its kind, and everything that creeps on the earth according to its kind. (Genesis 1:21,25)

Creation itself testifies *against* evolution. It screams *for* Intelligent Design. It confirms what the Bible tells us: every animal brings forth *after its own kind*. Unlike the theory of evolution, creationism fits with the scientific evidence and does not contradict any known scientific laws.

So far we've looked at only one scientific (knowledge-producing) evidence for the existence of God. Our marvelous creation provides *intellectual knowledge* that there must be a Creator. Now let's look at the next evidence for God's existence.

7

EVOLUTION'S STRANGE DILEMMA

"If I find in myself desires which nothing in this world can satisfy, the only logical explanation is that I was made for another world."

—C.S. Lewis

Here is another dilemma for the staunch atheist who embraces evolution. The theory of evolution asserts that everything evolved for a reason. We evolved arms because they provided an advantage. We evolved the skull, the eyes, nose, mouth, and ears because they served some purpose. The same applies to the brain, the reproductive organs, the liver, kidneys, lungs, and heart. We evolved the urge to sleep to rest us, an appetite to drive us to food, and thirst to drive us to water. Even within the human psyche we have evolved the emotion of fear to protect us, love to help us bond to the opposite sex for raising offspring, etc. All of these happened for our benefit, and so nothing evolved without a good reason.

So why then do the vast majority of human beings have an innate belief in the existence of God? Why did *that* evolve within the human need? The *New York Times* suggested an answer in March 2007, in an article by Robin Marantz Henig. Titled "Darwin's God," it offers "a scientific exploration of how we have come to believe in God."

The article is about Scott Atran, an anthropologist at the National Center for Scientific Research in Paris, who wrestled with questions about religion since he was ten years old. He no longer believes there is a God but he now struggles with "why so many other people, everywhere in the world, apparently do." Henig writes:

> Call it God; call it superstition; call it, as Atran does, "belief in hope beyond reason"—whatever you call it, there seems an inherent human drive to believe in something transcendent, unfathomable and otherworldly, something beyond the reach or understanding of science. "Why do we cross our fingers during turbulence, even the most atheistic among us?" asked Atran...
>
> Atran is Darwinian in his approach, which means he tries to explain behavior by how it might once have solved problems of survival and reproduction for our early ancestors. But it was not clear to him what evolutionary problems might have been solved by religious belief. Religion seemed

to use up physical and mental resources without an obvious benefit for survival. Why, he wondered, was religion so pervasive, when it was something that seemed so costly from an evolutionary point of view?[84]

Instead of being angered by the human belief in God, this scientist stands back thoughtfully, and—like a doctor objectively diagnosing the cause of a patient's condition—Atran studies the believer.

Richard Dawkins is not so philosophical. He believes that faith in God is nothing more than a useless, and sometimes dangerous, evolutionary accident. He says of the vast majority of humanity, "Religious behavior may be a misfiring, an unfortunate byproduct of an underlying psychological propensity which in other circumstances is, or once was, useful."

Other scientists think that belief in God is an outgrowth of brain architecture that evolved during early human history. What they can't agree on is why a tendency to believe actually evolved—whether it was because belief itself was adaptive or because it was just an evolutionary byproduct, a mere consequence of some other adaptation in the evolution of the human brain.

The *New York Times* article continues:

> Which is the better biological explanation for a belief in God—evolutionary adaptation or neurological accident? Is there something about the cognitive functioning

of humans that makes us receptive to belief in a super natural deity? And if scientists are able to explain God, what then? Is explaining religion the same thing as explaining it away? Are the nonbelievers right, and is religion at its core an empty undertaking, a misdirection, a vestigial artifact of a primitive mind? Or are the believers right, and does the fact that we have the mental capacities for discerning God suggest that it was God who put them there?

In short, are we hard-wired to believe in God? And if we are, how and why did that happen?[85]

Charles Darwin noted the tendency to believe in the supernatural in *The Descent of Man*. "A belief in all-pervading spiritual agencies," he wrote, "seems to be universal." Henig reports that, according to anthropologists, religions that share certain supernatural beliefs—belief in an immaterial God or gods, in the afterlife, and in the power of prayer—are found in virtually every culture on earth.

This universality certainly is true in the United States where 91 percent of adults say they believe in God.[86] Out of 6.5 billion people worldwide, only 2.36 percent are atheists.[87] But that's not surprising. Since God created us to be in relationship with Him, He would naturally have designed us so that we could believe in Him. We have hunger that can be satisfied with food; we have thirst that can be satisfied with water; we have desires for companionship, for love, for sexual intimacy, etc., because things exist that can satisfy these desires (not that we always get them, but they do exist). Likewise, we have a desire for God, because He exists to satisfy that desire.

And as the article mentions, even if evolutionists think they have found a rational explanation for belief, that doesn't mean we should stop believing. If science provides a physiological explanation for why I think my wife loves me, should I then stop believing that she does?

The article writer concludes:

> This internal push and pull between the spiritual and the rational reflects what used to be called the "God of the gaps" view of religion. The presumption was that *as science was able to answer more questions about the natural world, God would be invoked to answer fewer,* and religion would eventually recede. Research about the evolution of religion suggests otherwise. No matter how much science can explain, it seems, the real gap that God fills is an emptiness that our big-brained mental architecture interprets as a yearning for the supernatural. The drive to satisfy that yearning, according to both adaptationists and byproduct theorists, might be an inevitable and eternal part of what Atran calls the tragedy of human cognition.[88] (emphasis added)

To atheists, who find belief in God puzzling, there may seem to be a conflict between "the spiritual and the rational." But to the vast majority of people, belief is *very* rational. And as we've explored the scientific evidence, we've found that the evolutionists' presumptions have not been backed up by proof. Not only has science been unable to provide answers to where we came from, but the gaps they were seeking to fill have only widened exponentially.

In addition to the abundant external evidence of God in our world, we also have internal evidence of His existence in our mind. This "yearning for the supernatural" is given by God so that we might seek Him, and the only "tragedy" is when we ignore it.

With Knowledge

Aside from our universal disposition to believe that there is a God, all humankind has a conscience. The word "conscience" comes from two words and means "with knowledge" *(con* means "with" and *science* means "knowledge"). Here is the dictionary definition:

> Latin *conscientia,* "knowledge within oneself, a moral sense," "conscience," lit. "with-knowledge."[89]

With that in mind, consider the experience of a minister who went to Papua New Guinea, and met with a tribe that had no prior contact with Christianity. As he talked with them, he asked if they believed that certain things were wrong. For instance, he asked, "Do you believe that stealing is wrong?" They said, "Yes." When he asked if they believed cannibalism is wrong (some of them were practicing that), they said yes. He then asked others things, like, "Is adultery wrong?" and again they said yes. He asked them how they knew it was wrong, and they replied that they knew it in their being ... in their heart. That's the conscience. Here are people with no contact with the Bible, no contact with the Church, of any kind whatsoever, and yet instinctively they knew the difference between right and wrong.

Every human being has the moral Law written on his heart, and it speaks of issues of right and wrong. Some would argue that the conscience is a knowledge that comes by parental instruction or by society, while others believe that the conscience is pre-programmed by God. In other words, you are born with it. Because we find that certain activities like stealing, murder, and rape are considered wrong in cultures all around the world, the evidence points to the existence of a universal morality. You and I are "with knowledge" that some things are "right" and some things are "wrong" regardless of what was taught to us.

Consider for instance the case of two Australian schoolgirls who garroted a friend just to see what it was like to kill someone. In May 2007, following a drug-fueled party, the two

16-year-olds decided neither would feel bad about taking a life. So they stuffed a chemical-soaked cloth into the mouth of their 15-year-old friend, and throttled her with wire in a murder the judge called "gruesome and merciless in the extreme."

The girl who carried out the strangling told police she watched calmly as the emotions on her friend's face turned to terror when she realized they intended to kill her. Showing gross disregard for human life, they ignored their friend's pleas for her life. While the pair told authorities they were sorry about the impact of the murder on the victim's family, killing her "felt right" at the time.[90]

Did these girls do anything wrong? Hopefully, you said that their actions were morally wrong. If so, how do you know what they did was wrong? After all, it "felt right" to them to kill their friend. Do you think that they did wrong because your parents have taught you to think that way? What if Australia had no law against murder? Would it still be wrong? Could it ever be right? What if society determines that murdering your friends is actually "good" to further the human race, as long as those being murdered have low IQs, are handicapped, or are of a certain race or religion? I'm sure you feel as I do that no matter what your parents or your government may tell you, any form of murder is morally wrong.

The problem with atheism is that it has a shifting morality. There are no moral absolutes. How can there be, when morality is thought to come through human consensus, rather than divine mandate?

Human beings are unique among God's creation in that we are *moral* creatures. That's one of the many things that separate us from the animals—we have a distinctive knowledge of right and wrong, and so we set up court systems with punishment for wrongdoing. Unlike animals, we hold trials in which the evidence is presented before a jury. We want to ensure that fairness and justice prevail—especially when someone does something wrong against *us*.

We know right from wrong because the conscience is an impartial judge in the courtroom of the mind. It speaks to us irrespective of our will. Its voice can be so powerful that it has driven many men and women to drown themselves in alcohol, and some to a faster form of suicide.

Think about the machine that is commonly called a "lie detector." It's actually a polygraph machine—an instrument that monitors a person's physiological reactions. Unfortunately, it doesn't detect lies. Rather, it is a combination of medical devices that monitor changes occurring in the body when put under emotional stress.

As a person is questioned about a certain incident, the examiner looks to see the change in his heart rate, blood pressure, respiratory rate, and electro-dermal activity (sweatiness of his palms) in comparison to normal levels. Fluctuations may indicate that the person is lying, but exam results are open to interpretation by the examiner.

So why would a person's heart rate and blood pressure suddenly increase when answering certain questions? Why would he break out into a sweat? It's because he knows that he's guilty of not speaking the truth. That's what produces the physical reactions. So, the polygraph is actually trying to detect the workings of the human conscience and record the results. If the conscience is doing its work and producing a sense of guilt, it will be evidenced by a physical reaction.

> *The polygraph is actually trying to detect the workings of the human conscience and record the results.*

Regardless of whether we follow it, we all have an internal knowledge that it is wrong to lie, steal, murder, and commit adultery. While we don't need to read the Bible to know that these things are wrong or that we have a conscience, it is interesting to consider what the all-time bestselling book says regarding this "moral compass." It states that the problem with the human conscience is that it has been "seared." That is, it has lost its life on the outside and become calloused. Like a smoke detector whose batteries are weak, it no longer functions properly. Accordingly, God has designed something to bring the conscience back to life so it can do its duty. The way to bring life back into the conscience is to look to the moral Law—Ten Commandments.

The Commandments are like a mirror. When you and I got up this morning, one of the first things we did was look into the mirror. Why did we do that? We wanted to see what damage had been done during the night.

The mirror doesn't clean us. All it does is reflect the truth so that we can see ourselves for what we are, and that motivates us to get things fixed up before we go into public.

So with that thought in mind, let's look into the mirror of God's moral Law and see what it does to us. It may not be a pretty sight—you may want to look away—but please be patient, because it is a very powerful tool in helping you discover the reality of God's existence.

The Self-Test

The goal in completing this self-examination is to simply stir your conscience so that it will do its God-given duty. If you harden your heart, you will not hear its voice.

First, have you ever told a lie? I'm not talking about using discretion; I'm talking about a bold-faced lie. If you have lied even once, what does that make you? It makes you a liar. The Bible tells us, "Lying lips are an abomination to the LORD,"[91] because He is a God of truth and holiness.

Have you ever stolen anything? The value of the item is irrelevant. If you have, then you are a thief. Have you ever used God's name in vain? If you have, then you have taken the name of the God who gave you life and used it as a filth word to express disgust. That's called blasphemy, and it's understandably a very serious offense in His sight. (We don't even use the name of Hitler, who killed six million innocent people, as a curse word.) The Bible says that God will not hold him guiltless who takes His name in vain.

Jesus said, "Whoever looks at a woman to lust for her has already committed adultery with her in his heart."[92] Have you ever looked with lust at someone other than your spouse (this includes sex outside of marriage)? If you have violated those four Laws, then by your own admission, you are a lying, thieving, blasphemous, adulterer at heart, and you have to face God on Judgment Day. And that's only four of the Ten Commandments. Let's quickly look at the other six.

Is God first in your life, above all else? He should be. He's given you your life and everything that is dear to you. Do you love Him with *all* of your heart, soul, mind, and strength? That's the requirement of the First Commandment. Or have you broken the Second Commandment by making a god in your mind that you're comfortable with—where you say, "My god is a loving and merciful god who would never send anyone to Hell"? That god doesn't exist; he's a figment of your imagination. To create a god in your mind (your own image of God) is something the Bible calls idolatry. Idolaters will not enter Heaven.

Have you always honored your parents implicitly, and kept the Sabbath holy? If not, you have broken the Fourth and Fifth Commandments. Have you ever hated someone? The Bible says, "Whoever hates his brother is a murderer."[93] Have you coveted (jealously desired) other people's things? This is a violation of the Tenth Commandment.

So here is the crucial question: If God judges you by the moral Law on Judgment Day, will you be found innocent or guilty of breaking this Law? *Think before you answer.* Would you go to Heaven or Hell?

Perhaps the thought of going to Hell doesn't alarm you, because you don't believe in it. That may be your belief, but if Hell exists, your lack of belief won't make it go away. Standing on a freeway and saying, "I don't believe in trucks" won't make the eighteen-wheeler disappear.

According to recent polls, the majority of Americans *do* believe in a literal place called Hell.[94] Most people think that it's a fitting place for Hitler and other mass murderers—and they're right. Because God is good, He will make sure that murderers get what's coming to them. That makes sense. But He's not only good, He's *perfect,* and His justice is going to be very thorough. God will also punish rapists, adulterers, pedophiles, fornicators, blasphemers, hypocrites, thieves, and liars. We are told in the Bible that all liars will have their part in the Lake of Fire, and thieves and adulterers will not inherit the Kingdom of Heaven. Think about it—if God's standards are that high, that leaves us all in big trouble.

But He also sees our *thought-life,* and He will judge us for the hidden sins of the heart: for lust, hatred, rebellion, greed, unclean imaginations, ingratitude, selfishness, jealousy, pride, envy, deceit, etc. Jesus warned, "But I say to you that for *every idle word* men may speak, they will give account of it in the day of judgment"[95] (emphasis added). The Bible says that God's wrath abides on each of us, and that every time we sin, we're storing up wrath that will be revealed on Judgment Day.

Does that concern you? Is your conscience speaking to you? Is it accusing you of being guilty? Thank you for your patience and honesty with this section, as this is a difficult subject to consider. Hopefully your conscience has been awakened. You should now recognize the danger of your predicament. The just penalty of sin—breaking even one Law—is death, and eternity in Hell. But you haven't broken just one Law. Like the rest of us, you've no doubt broken all of these laws, countless times each. What kind of anger do you think a judge is justified in having toward a criminal guilty of breaking the Law *thousands of times?*

So what should you do? Turn to religion? But there are so many—which one should you choose? Please stay with me. We'll look at the answer to this crucial question next.

8

THE FOUR GIFTS

"There are only two kinds of men: the righteous, who believe themselves sinners; the rest, sinners, who believe themselves righteous."

—Blaise Pascal

Let's say you are convinced that God exists, and you realize you will have to face Him on Judgment Day. But you are not sure which religion to follow to be right with God. Each religion has a different teaching about God, so while they can all be wrong, they can't all be right. Let me show you why Christianity is unique among religions.[96]

Imagine I offered you a choice of four gifts:
- The original Mona Lisa
- The keys to a brand new Lamborghini
- Ten million dollars in cash
- A parachute

You can pick only one. Which would you choose? Before you decide, here's some information that will help you to make the wisest choice: *You have to jump 10,000 feet out of an airplane.*

Does that help you to connect the dots? It should, because you *need* the parachute. It's the only one of the four gifts that will help with your dilemma. The others may have some value, but they are useless when it comes to facing the law of gravity in a 10,000-foot fall. The knowledge that you will have to jump should produce a healthy fear in you—and that kind of fear is good because it can save your life. Remember that.

Now think of the four major religions:
- Hinduism
- Buddhism
- Islam
- Christianity

Which one should you choose? Before you decide, here's some information that will help you determine which one is the wisest choice: All of humanity stands on the edge of eternity. We are *all* going to die. We will all have to pass through the door of death. It could happen to us in twenty years, or in six months ... or today. For most of humanity, death is a huge and terrifying plummet into the unknown. So what should we do?

Do you remember how it was your knowledge of the law of gravity that produced that healthy fear, and that fear helped you to make the best choice? You know what the law of gravity can do to you at 10,000 feet. In the same way, your knowledge of the moral Law will hopefully help you make the best choice with life's greatest issue—what happens when you die.

The Bible tells us that when we take that "unknown leap" and pass through the door of death, we have to face "the law of sin and death"—the Ten Commandments. As we have seen, we are without excuse when we stand before God because He gave us our conscience to know right from wrong. Each time we lie, steal, commit adultery, and so on, we know that it is wrong.

As we have looked at this subject, you may have developed a sense of fear. Remember to let that fear work for your good. The fear of God is the healthiest fear you can have. The Bible calls it "the beginning of wisdom."[97]

Let's now look at those four major religions to see which one, if any, can help you with your predicament.

Hinduism: The religion of Hinduism says that if you've been bad, you may come back as a rat or some other animal.[98] If you've been good, you might come back as a prince. But that's like someone saying, "When you jump out of the plane, you'll get sucked back in as another passenger. If you've been bad, you go down to the Economy Class; if you've been good, you go up to First Class."

> *For most of humanity, death is a huge and terrifying plummet into the unknown. So what should we do?*

It's an interesting concept, but it doesn't deal with your real problem of having sinned against God and the reality of Hell. And there is no evidence for this belief.

Buddhism: Amazingly, the religion of Buddhism denies that God even exists. It says that life and death are sort of an illusion.[99] That's like standing at the door of the plane and saying, "I'm not really here, and there's no such thing as the law of gravity, and no ground that I'm going to hit." That may temporarily help you deal with your fears, but it doesn't square with reality. And it doesn't deal with your real problem of having sinned against God and the reality of Hell.

Islam: Interestingly, Islam acknowledges the reality of sin and Hell, and the justice of God, but the hope it offers is that sinners can escape God's justice if they do religious works. God will see these, *and because of them,* hopefully He will show mercy—but they won't know for sure.[100] Each person's works will be weighed on the Day of Judgment and it will then be decided who is saved and who is not—based on whether they followed Islam, were sincere in repentance, and performed enough righteous deeds to outweigh their bad ones.

So Islam believes you can earn God's mercy by your own efforts. But that's like jumping out of the plane, and believing that flapping your arms is going to counter the law of gravity and save you from a 10,000-foot drop.

And there's something else to consider. The Law of God shows us that even the best of us is nothing more than a condemned criminal, standing guilty and without excuse before the throne of a perfect and holy Judge. When that is understood, then our "righteous deeds" are actually seen as an attempt to bribe the Judge of the Universe. The Bible says that because of our guilt, anything we offer God for our justification (to get ourselves off the hook) is an abomination to Him.[101] Islam, like the other religions, cannot save you from the consequences of sinning against God.

Christianity: So why is Christianity different? Aren't all religions the same? Let's see. In Christianity, God Himself provided a "parachute" for us, and the Bible tells us regarding the Savior, "Put on the Lord Jesus Christ."[102] Just as a parachute solved your dilemma with the law of gravity and its consequences, so the Savior perfectly solves your dilemma with the Law of God and its consequences! It is the missing puzzle-piece that you need.

How did God solve our dilemma? He satisfied His wrath by becoming a human being and taking our punishment upon Himself. The Scriptures tell us that God was in Christ, reconciling the world to Himself. Christianity provides the only parachute to save us from the consequences of the Law we have transgressed.

Back to the Plane

In looking at the four major religions to see if they can help us in our dilemma, we find that Christianity fits the bill perfectly. To illustrate this more clearly, let's go back to that plane for a moment. You are standing on the edge of a 10,000-foot drop. You have to jump. Your heart is thumping in your chest. Why? Because you know that the law of gravity will kill you when you jump.

Someone offers you the original Mona Lisa. You push it aside.

Another person passes you the keys to a brand new Lamborghini. You let them drop to the floor.

Someone else tries to put ten million dollars into your hands. You push the hand away, and stand there in horror at your impending fate.

> It is your knowledge of the law of gravity and your fear of the jump that turns you toward the good news of the parachute.

Suddenly, you hear a voice say, "Here's a parachute!"

Which one of those four people is going to hold the most credibility in your eyes? It's the one who held up the parachute! Again, it is your knowledge of the law of gravity and your fear of the jump that turns you toward the good news of the parachute.

In the same way, knowledge of what God's moral Law will do to you on the Day of Judgment produces a fear that makes the gospel unspeakably good news! It solves your predicament of God's wrath. God became a sinless human being in the person of Jesus of Nazareth. The Savior died an excruciating death on the cross, taking your punishment (the death penalty) upon Himself, and the demands of eternal justice were satisfied the moment He cried, "It is finished!" The Bible tells us, "Christ has redeemed us from the curse of the law, having been made a curse for us."[103] We broke the Law, but God became a man to pay our penalty with His own life's blood.

Then He rose from the dead, defeating death. This means that God can forgive every sin you have ever committed and commute your death sentence. When you repent (turn from your sins) and place your faith in Jesus Christ, you can say with the apostle Paul:

> For the law of the Spirit of life in Christ Jesus has made me free from the law of sin and death.[104]

So you no longer need to be afraid of death, and you don't need to look any further for ways to make peace between you and God. The Savior is God's gift to you. It is unspeakably good news!

Now God Himself can "justify" you. He can wash you clean and give you the "righteousness" of Christ. He can save you from death and Hell, and grant you everlasting life—something that you could never earn or deserve.

If you haven't yet repented and trusted the Savior, please do it now. Tell God you are sorry for your sins, then *turn* from them, and place your trust in Jesus Christ alone to save you. Don't wait until tomorrow. It may never come.

The Immigration Department

Rick is my plumber. Each time we needed to have something fixed at the ministry or at my home, I grew to know him better and like him more. That's because Rick is a nice guy—a typical genuine Christian. He has a warm personality, and is friendly and hardworking.

One day Rick told me that he was taking his family to New Zealand for a vacation. I was thrilled. New Zealand is my home country, and it really is beautiful. He was flying 7,000 miles from Los Angeles to the city of Auckland and then driving to the Bay of Islands for some snorkeling and deep-sea fishing.

A short time later he was back. He explained that, while flying into Auckland, his wife filled out the necessary customs and immigration forms. Her eyes fell on one question on her husband's form. It asked, "Have you been arrested?" She hesitated. Rick had spent time in jail before he was a Christian. Then she answered yes.

An hour or so later, they arrived in Auckland and excitedly went through the entrance procedure. As he waited at customs, an officer looked at the checked box on the declaration card. He looked at Rick and said, "You will need to speak with immigration." Immigration told him that they needed to ask him a few questions. It was nothing personal, but they had to write down everything he said. It was a very mechanical process. Why had he been arrested? It was for burglary, to support a drug habit. How long had he spent in jail? More than a year. Would he use drugs in New Zealand?

Rick politely answered all of their questions, and even shared the gospel with them. He had to, because they asked him how he was able to break his drug habit. They then left him for a short time, returned and said that in 1978 New Zealand had passed a law prohibiting anyone who had been in jail for more than 12 months from entering New Zealand. They were very sorry, but it was not negotiable. He had to return to the United States.

Rick went back to his wife and kids and told them the bad news. They would have to go on without him. The family cried bitterly together, and then they separated.

When I found out what had happened, I was both embarrassed and angry. How could my home country treat my friend so horribly! As a

Christian, Rick was now a new person. What's more, he was honest enough to admit the truth about his past. I wanted to complain to someone, but I couldn't ... because New Zealand had the right to set its own standards of entry.

Heaven has done the same. No lawbreaker will ever enter its gates. Not a soul. So if you want to avoid Hell, it would be wise for you to check out the standard of entry into Heaven, before you try to get in. Here it is:

> There shall by no means enter it anything that defiles, or causes an abomination or a lie, but only those who are written in the Lamb's Book of Life ... But the cowardly, unbelieving, abominable, murderers, sexually immoral, sorcerers, idolaters, and all liars shall have their part in the lake which burns with fire and brimstone, which is the second death. (Revelation 21:8, 21:27)

However, unlike with New Zealand, there is a way to have your criminal record permanently expunged—completely removed so you have a clean record. In addition to having your past washed away, you can become a brand new person.

He Made a Way

The Bible tells us that this same Judge who will find you guilty of breaking His Law is also rich in mercy. He has made a way for you to be forgiven. "For God so loved the world that He gave His only begotten Son, that whoever believes in Him should not perish but have everlasting life."[105]

If there was one chance in a million that this is true, you owe it to your good sense to consider it with an open heart. God offers everlasting life to all humanity, and promises, "Their sins and their lawless deeds I will remember no more" (Hebrews 10:17). What you must do in response is to "re pent" (not simply confess your sins, but *turn* from them), and trust the Savior (not just a belief, but a "trust"—as you would trust a parachute to save you). The moment you do that, *God reveals Himself to you*—not in a vision or in a voice, but He does so by giving you His Holy Spirit to live inside you. He makes you brand new on the inside, so that you want to do that which is pleasing to Him.

That's a miracle for a sin-loving sinner like me. That happened to me on April 25, 1972, at 1:30 in the morning, and after all these years I am still shaking my head at the radical nature of my conversion. It's so radical that the Bible calls it being "born again." In one moment I was made a new person.

It's like this. If I look at a heater and *believe* the heater is hot, I have an intellectual belief. But if I say to myself, "I wonder if it really *is* hot" and reach out and grip the bar, the second my flesh burns, I stop *believing* it's hot, I now *know* it's hot. I have moved out of the realm of *belief* into the realm of *experience*.

That's what will happen to you the moment you are born again (when you become a Christian). You will move out of the realm of "belief" into the realm of "personal experience." A Christian is not someone who has a "belief," but someone who has a relationship with the living God. You come to *know* Him. You will say with the writer of "Amazing Grace," "I once was blind, but now I see."

9

THREE WISE FOOLS

"God has given us evidence sufficiently clear to convince those with an open heart and mind..."

—Blaise Pascal

There once were three men who considered that they were very wise. They lived in a country that had only just been introduced to electricity.

One dark night, the men were invited by Edison Electric to see a demonstration of electrical power, because it was well-known that the three of them were skeptical about the reality of electricity. They denied its existence because they didn't believe in anything that they couldn't see with their own eyes. These men were rationalists, and electricity was said to be invisible.

When they entered the dimly lit demonstration room, they were cordially met by a representative from Edison Electric. As they looked around, they saw that a large lamp sat on a table in the middle of the room. Also on the table were a candle and a leather-bound book called *The Owner's Manual*, published by the electric company.

The representative welcomed them and excitedly explained that the lamp had the power to illuminate a large area, with the simple flick of a switch.

He said, "Gentlemen, electricity is a modern marvel. To see it demonstrated, simply flick the switch on the lamp. You will be amazed. It will light up the entire room. The manual on the table will give you further instruction."

He then left the room to speak with other interested clients.

All the men needed to do to see the miracle of electricity was to flick the switch on the lamp.

Instead, they sat down at the table, and one of them opened *The Owner's Manual* and began to cynically look at its pages. It began with a short biographical sketch of the famous inventor Thomas Edison.

The chapters contained the following:
- A diagram of the position of the switch on the lamp
- Background information on how electricity was discovered
- Pictures of huge dams with descriptions of how they are able to turn raw energy from moving water into hydroelectric power
- Diagrams of copper wiring and magnets, explaining how they produce electricity
- Explanation of how electrical wiring carries the generated power to our homes

- Illustrations of electrical sockets, power cords, and other accessories

As the man continued to flip through its pages, it was as though the lamp that sat on the table in front of them didn't exist. Then they began to talk. The conversation went like this:

"I don't believe that there is any such thing as 'electricity.' I've never seen it. It's supposed to be invisible and yet produce light. How ridiculous! Where's the evidence? If I can't see it, it doesn't exist."

"I totally agree," said the man holding the book. "It says here on page 17 that Edison was considered to be a genius. I don't think so. I've studied his life and he had so many failures, it was ridiculous. He didn't even invent the light bulb—several other people beat him to it.

"Who published this book anyway? I doubt if they know anything about Thomas Edi son. I notice here that it says that his wife's name was Mary Stilwell. That's just not true. I'm an educated man. I did a thesis on the man's life once, and I know that his wife's name was definitely Mina."

"Interesting ... I read somewhere that he used this so-called 'electricity' to kill animals. Is that true?"

The man holding the book said, "It's true. There has been a great deal of evil done in the name of this so-called 'electricity.' That's why I don't want to have anything to do with it.

"The mess-up with his wife's name isn't the only mistake in this publication. It says here that Edison was an atheist. That's absurd! I have read many times that he believed in God's existence. This manual is a mess. It's filled with contradictions.

"And they expect us to believe in this invisible force called 'electricity'—that has to be the dumbest thing I have ever heard! I don't know about you, but I'm getting out of here."

His two friends heartily agreed. Electricity wasn't real. It seemed to make sense to them that it didn't exist because they believed that *The Owner's Manual* was filled with mistakes.

The three men stepped out of the room into the darkness, still wise in their own eyes. They even decided to form a club that was devoted to telling other people that electricity didn't exist.

Flick the Switch

Sadly, it seems the men had only half of the information—and so they came to the wrong conclusions.

It's true that Edison didn't invent the light bulb; among hundreds of other inventions, he's credited with creating the first commercially practical incandescent light. After his first wife, Mary Stilwell, died, Edison married Mina Miller. And he did electrocute animals—most notably an elephant whose owner wanted it put to death after it killed several people—but only to demonstrate the dangers of AC power.

Although Edison is quoting as saying, "I believe that the science of chemistry alone almost proves the existence of an intelligent creator," he also stated, "What you call God I call Nature, the Supreme intelligence that rules matter." For all his brilliance, Edison believed that "nature made us—nature did it all—not the gods of the religions."

The reason many atheists give for unbelief is that they are either offended by hypocrisy (atrocities done in the name of God) or by what they see as mistakes in the Bible. To date, I have been reading the Bible every day without fail for thirty-five years. I have yet to come across even one error in the Word of God.

These facts are available to any who want to find them.

To discover the reality of electricity, all these men had to do was flick the switch in order to actually *see* *the light*. They had all the proof they would ever need that electricity exists—if they were genuinely interested in knowing the truth.

Here's the essence of what I'm saying. If you will seek God's forgiveness through the gospel, He promises to personally reveal Himself to *you*. That's your ultimate proof. My personal experience cannot prove anything to you (because I could be lying or be deluded), but if *you* experience the life-changing power of the Holy Spirit of God, it will be all the proof you need!

In other words, don't just take my word for it; call on the name of the Lord yourself. Flick the switch.

Conversion is more than a change of heart, a change of mind, or a change of philosophy. It is far more than a feeling, an experience, or a vision.

> *If you will seek God's forgiveness through the gospel, He promises to personally reveal Himself to you. That's your ultimate proof.*

The Bible promises that the moment you are converted you will receive power when the Holy Spirit comes upon you. We are also told that when the gospel came, it came "in power, in the Holy Spirit ... and in much assurance." You will radically pass from death to life, from darkness to light, from the kingdom of Satan to the Kingdom of God. You will truly be born again, and God will give you a new heart and new desires.

So, what would drive you to actually take that step to repent and trust the Savior? Maybe you can think of a hundred reasons why you shouldn't—it doesn't make sense, what would your friends think, what would you have to give up, etc.

Here's one very good reason why you should: you are part of the ultimate statistic—ten out of ten people die. If you are sane, there is something inside of you that is saying, "I don't want to die!" That's your God-given will to live. Please listen to it. Our hunger for food is given to us by God so that we could carry on living. How foolish we would be to ignore it and starve to death. Our will to live is also God-given. It is an insatiable hunger to live that should drive us to set aside our pride and seek the immortality that God offers humanity.

Let your fear of death open your heart to the claims of the gospel.

10

THIS DAY WAS DIFFERENT

"I find more sure marks of authenticity in the Bible than in any profane history whatsoever."

—Sir Isaac Newton

As we have seen in the previous chapter, atheists approach the Bible with a "darkened understanding" (see Ephesians 4:18) and try to make sense of it. But just as the Bible says, they cannot understand it (see 1 Corinthians 2:14). The only way the Scriptures can make sense to us is for us to read them with a humble heart that is searching for truth. God promises to resist those who are proud.

Obviously, the best way for anyone to understand God's Word is to switch on the light—to repent and trust Him who said, "I am the light of the world. He who follows Me shall not walk in darkness, but have the light of life" (John 8:12).

It is legitimate, though, to ask: How can we know the Bible is divinely inspired? The Bible declares that it is the Word of God, His communication to humanity, so He certainly would give us evidence that it truly is His Word. The fulfilled prophecies, the amazing consistency, and the many scientific statements of the Bible provide evidence that it is supernatural in origin. We will look at some examples, and then we'll consider what it is that gives even more credibility to the reality of God and the inspiration of the Scriptures.

Knowledge of the Future

Unlike other books, the Bible offers a multitude of specific predictions—some thousands of years in advance—that either have been literally fulfilled or point to a definite future time when they will come true. No other religion has specific, repeated, and unfailing fulfillment of predictions many years in advance of events over which the predictor had no control. The sacred writings of Buddhism, Islam, Confucius, etc., are all missing the element of proven prophecy. These kinds of predictions are unique to the Bible.

Only one who is omniscient can accurately predict details of events thousands of years in the future. Limited human beings know the future only if it is told to them by an omniscient Being. God provided this evidence for us so we would know that the Scriptures have a divine Author:

"For I am God, and there is no other;
I am God, and there is none like Me,

declaring the end from the beginning, and from ancient times things that are not yet done." (Isaiah 46:9,10)

In addition, the Bible declares that prophets must be 100 percent accurate—no exceptions. If anyone claimed to be speaking for God and the prophesied event didn't come to pass, he was proven to be a liar. The writings of Mormons and Jehovah's Witnesses are littered with false prophecies, so we know can whether they are written by men or by God.

The Bible's sixty-six books, written between 1400B.C. and A.D.90, contain approximately 3,856 verses concerned with prophecy. For example, the Scriptures predicted the rise and fall of great empires like Greece and Rome (Daniel 2:39,40), and foretold the destruction of cities like Tyre and Sidon (Isaiah 23). Tyre's demise is recorded by ancient historians, who tell how Alexander the Great lay siege to the city for seven months. King Nebuchadnezzar of Babylon had failed in a 13-year attempt to capture the seacoast city and completely destroy its inhabitants. During the siege of 573B.C., much of the population of Tyre moved to its new island home half a mile from the land city. Here it remained surrounded by walls as high as 150 feet until judgment fell in 332B.C. with the arrival of Alexander the Great. In the seven-month siege, he fulfilled the remainder of the prophecies (Zechariah 9:4; Ezekiel 26:12) concerning the city at sea by completely destroying Tyre, killing 8,000 of its inhabitants and selling 30,000 of its population into slavery. To reach the island, he scraped up the dust and rubble of the old land city of Tyre, just like the Bible predicted, and cast them into the sea, building a 200-foot-wide causeway out to the island.

> *Only one who is omniscient can accurately predict details of events thousands of years in the future.*

Alexander's death and the murder of his two sons were also foretold in the Scripture. Another startling prophecy was Jesus' detailed prediction of Jerusalem's destruction, and the further dispersion of Jews throughout the world, which is recorded in Luke 21. In A.D.70, not only was Jerusalem destroyed by Titus, the future emperor of Rome, but another prediction of Jesus' in Matthew 24:1,2 came to pass—the complete destruction of the temple of God.

Even more important are the many prophecies of a coming Messiah. God said He would send someone to redeem mankind from sin, and He wanted there to be no mistake about who that Person would be. For example, in the Book of Daniel, the Bible prophesied the coming of the one and only Jewish Messiah prior to the temple's demise. The Old Testament prophets declared He would be born in Bethlehem (Micah 5:2) to a virgin (Isaiah 7:14), be betrayed for thirty pieces of silver (Zechariah 11:12,13), die by crucifixion (Psalm 22), and be buried in a rich man's tomb (Isaiah 53:9). There was only one person who fits all of the messianic prophecies of the Old Testament: Jesus of Nazareth, the Son of Mary. In all, there are over three hundred prophecies that tell of the ancestry, birth, life, ministry, death, resurrection, and ascension of Jesus of Nazareth. All have been literally fulfilled to the smallest detail.

A fact often overlooked by critics is that, even if most biblical predictions could be explained naturally, the existence of just one real case of fulfilled prophecy is sufficient to establish the Bible's supernatural origin. Over 25 percent of the entire Bible contains specific predictive prophecies that have been literally fulfilled. This is true of no other book in the world. And it is a sure sign of its divine origin.

Knowledge of Creation

Following are a few examples of incredible scientific facts that were written in the Bible, hundreds, even thousands of years before man discovered them.

At a time when it was commonly believed that the earth sat on a large animal or a giant (1500B.C.), the Bible spoke of the earth's free float in space: "He hangs the earth on nothing" (Job 26:7). Science didn't discover that the earth hangs on nothing until 1650.

The Scriptures tell us that the earth is round: "It is He who sits above the circle of the earth" (Isaiah 40:22). The word translated "circle" here is the Hebrew word *chuwg*, which is also translated "circuit" or "compass" (depending on the con text). That is, it indicates something spherical or rounded—not flat or square. The Book of Isaiah was written between 740 and 680B.C. This is at least 300 years before Aristotle suggested, in his book *On the Heavens*, that the earth might be a sphere. It was another 2,000 years later (at a time when science believed that the earth was flat) that the Scriptures inspired Christopher Columbus to sail around the world.

Matthew Maury (1806–1873) is considered the father of oceanography. He noticed the expression "paths of the seas" in Psalm 8:8 (written 2,800 years ago) and stated, "If God said there are paths in the sea, I am going to find them." Maury then took God at His word and went looking for these paths, and we are indebted to him for his discovery of the warm and cold continental currents. His book on oceanography remains a basic text on the subject and is still used in universities.

Only in recent years has science discovered that everything we see is composed of things that we cannot see—invisible atoms. In Hebrews 11:3, written 2,000 years ago, Scripture tells us that the "things which are seen were not made of things which are visible."

Three different places in the Bible (Isaiah 51:6; Psalm 102:25,26; Hebrews 1:11) indicate that the earth is wearing out. This is what the Second Law of Thermodynamics (the Law of Increasing Entropy) states: that in all physical processes, every ordered system over time tends to become more disordered. Everything is running down and wearing out as energy is becoming less and less available for use. That means the universe will eventually "wear out" to the extent that (theoretically speaking) there will be a "heat death" and therefore no more energy available for use. This wasn't discovered by science until recently, but the Bible states it in concise terms.

The Scriptures inform us, "All the rivers run into the sea, yet the sea is not full; to the place from which the rivers come, there they return again" (Ecclesiastes 1:7). This statement alone may not seem profound. But when considered with other biblical passages, it becomes all the more remarkable. For example, the Mississippi River dumps approximately 518 billion gallons of water every 24 hours into the Gulf of Mexico. Where does all that water go? And that's just one of thousands of rivers. The answer lies in the hydrologic cycle, so well brought out in the Bible. Ecclesiastes 11:3 states that "if the clouds are full of rain, they empty themselves upon the earth." Look at the Bible's words in Amos 9:6: "He ... calls for the waters of the sea, and pours them out on the face of the earth." The idea of a complete water cycle was not fully understood by science until the seventeenth century. However, more than two thousand years prior to the discoveries of Pierre Perrault, Edme Mariotte, Edmund Halley, and others, the Scriptures clearly spoke of a water cycle.

The Scriptures also describe a "cycle" of air currents two thousand years before scientists discovered them: "The wind goes toward the south, and turns around to the north; the wind whirls about continually, and comes again on its circuit" (Ecclesiastes 1:6). We now know that air around the earth turns in huge circles, clockwise in one hemisphere and counterclockwise in the other.

The Bible declares, "Thus the heavens and the earth, and all the host of them, were finished" (Genesis 2:1). The original Hebrew uses the past definite tense for the verb "finished," indicating an action completed in the past, never again to occur. The creation was "finished"—once and for all. That is exactly what the First Law of Thermodynamics says. This law (often referred to as the Law of the Conservation of Energy and/or Mass) states that neither matter nor energy can be either created or destroyed. It was because of this Law that Sir Fred Hoyle's "Steady-State" (or "Continuous Creation") Theory was discarded. Hoyle stated that at points in the universe called "irtrons," matter (or energy) was constantly being created. But, the First Law states just the opposite. Indeed, there is no "creation" ongoing today. It is "finished" exactly as the Bible states.

In Genesis 6, God gave Noah the dimensions of the 1.5 million cubic foot ark he was to build. In 1609 at Hoorn in Holland, a ship was built after that same pattern (30:5:3), revolutionizing ship-building. By 1900 every large ship on the high seas was inclined toward the proportions of the ark (verified by "Lloyd's Register of Shipping" in the *World Almanac*).

Since God is the Author of creation as well as the Bible, it's only natural that the two should correspond. While the Bible is not intended to be a scientific book, the scientific statements it makes are accurate. In his book *Proofs of God's Existence*, Richard Wurmbrand explains:

> In antiquity and in what is called the Dark Ages, men did not know what they now know about humanity and the cosmos. They did not know the lock but they possessed the key, which is God. Now many have excellent descriptions of the lock but they have lost the key. The proper solution is union between religion and science. We should be owners of the lock and the key. The fact is that as science advances, it discovers what was said thousands of years ago in the Bible.[106]

There Is Another Way

I know that many who read through the above evidences of the Bible being divinely inspired will disregard them. They maintain that we are reading into Scripture something that was never intended by the writers. So, in an effort to counter this reaction, I am going to present my case from another angle.

What I am going to say flies in the face of many respected Bible teachers. It almost sounds like heresy, but I will say it anyway because it's important. The Christian's salvation isn't dependent on his belief in or understanding of the Scriptures. Why does that fly in the face of many? Because they believe that our salvation depends on the Word of God. They believe that everything we have in Christ stands or falls on the promises of the Bible. The Scriptures are the foundation for our faith. While I absolutely believe that the Bible is the Word of God, and that all Scripture is given by inspiration of God, I don't believe our salvation stands or falls on our believing the Bible.

> *While I absolutely believe that the Bible is the Word of God, I don't believe our salvation stands or falls on our believing the Bible.*

To illustrate this, let's look at two men who are in a Russian dungeon. One is a Christian who has been horribly tortured for his faith. As he lies dying in his cell, he shares his faith with his unbelieving cellmate. The other prisoner is a bitter man who so despised Christians that he hadn't spoken to him since they were forced to share the tiny cell. But this day was different. He listens intently to the dying man's words, because he is on his deathbed. Through parched lips the Christian once again whispers the Ten Commandments, showing sin to be very serious in the sight of God. The man becomes deeply concerned as his conscience begins to bear witness to what he is hearing.[107] The moral Law shows him that he has a serious problem with God's wrath.[108] There is no talk of a God-shaped hole in his heart, a wonderful plan for his life, or the promise of any benefits of faith in Jesus during this life. How could the Christian talk of a "wonderful plan" that so many speak of, while he lies dying because he had been beaten for his faith?

The prisoner listens as he is told that he is a desperately wicked criminal who needs forgiveness from the God he has greatly angered. Then he hears the pure gospel of the love of God in Christ, and of the necessity of repentance and faith. He hears of the One who can wash him clean. It answers his problem of coming wrath of which he is now convinced. The Christian then pleads with him to repent, breaths his last, and passes into eternity.

The prisoner is left alone in the cold cell. He is shaken by what he has just heard. He falls to his knees on the hard floor and trembles before God. He can hardly lift his head because of the weight of his sins. In humble contrition, he openly confesses his many transgressions against God's Law. He pleads for mercy, repents, and places his entire trust in Jesus Christ for his eternal salvation. He has no Bible. He has no fellowship. He has no one to "follow up" with him. He is entirely alone.

The next day he wakens while still lying on the floor. As he opens his tired eyes, something is different. Something is *radically* different. There is a new song in his heart. It's not a "song" that he could sing, but it's some sort of a joy that he can hardly express. He also has a sense of peace that is beyond his comprehension. He has never felt these emotions before, and what is mystifying is that he has no reason to feel this joy. He is tired, alone, and hungry, in a cold dungeon. He also notices that he is no longer ashamed to lift his head to the heavens. In fact, he *wants* to speak to God in prayer.

But more than that, he has an overwhelming desire to please Him more than anything else in his life. He even notices that his nagging conscience was silenced and *any* sense of guilt about any of his past sins is gone. He is amazed at what he has experienced. Again, nothing like this has ever happened before—not for a fleeting moment in his bitter, godless years. Never. God was the last thing on his mind.

He then looks at the lifeless body of the cellmate he once despised, and longs to speak with him. He wants to ask for his forgiveness. He wants to talk about the God who made Himself known to him, the God who forgave him for his sins ... the God who loved him enough to send His Son to die for him.

This was more than some sort of subjective experience. He was a brand new person with a new heart and new desires. Tears filled his eyes as he thought of the cross of Jesus Christ. Oh, that wonderful cross! Jesus of Nazareth had suffered and died for him! Then He defeated death. The man's heart almost burst with joy.

After five more years of solitary confinement, our prisoner has grown in his faith. He has preached the gospel to hardened guards. He has told them of the standard of perfection with which God would judge them, opening up the Ten Commandments. He has faithfully shared the reality of Judgment Day and the terrors of an eternal Hell. He preaches that Christ was crucified for the sin of the world, and stresses the necessity of repentance and faith. The guards taunt him regularly, and now and then beat him. He, in return, prays earnestly for their salvation. He also prays for the salvation of his family, and for the world. He continually worships God and lives a life of holiness, free from sin, trusting minute by minute in the finished work of Calvary's cross.

Notice that he is a Christian. He is born again. He knows that he has passed from death to life. He is a believer who is strong in his faith *and he has not yet even seen a Bible* or spoken to another Christian. His faith rests on the fact that God made him a new creature, wrote His Law on his heart and caused him to walk in His statutes.[109] He is a new person, a "new man which was created according to God, in true righteousness and holiness."[110] Old things passed away and all things became new.[111] This is because He was born of God.[112]

The New Testament didn't convert him. It is the *gospel* that is the power of God to salvation.[113] Neither did the New Testament spiritually feed him. He now has the Spirit of God living within him to guide him into all truth.[114] His faith wasn't in the Scriptures, or a church, or a pastor, or another Christian. It wasn't in his good works or in his religion. It was the fact that he was a new creature that convinced him of the reality of God. The New Testament addresses this thought: "For in Christ Jesus neither circumcision nor uncircumcision avails anything, but *a new creation*"[115] (emphasis added).

The Explanation Book

One day, a sympathetic guard slips the prisoner a battered and well-used New Testament that once belonged to his deceased cellmate. The prisoner doesn't even know what "The New Testament" is. He wasn't aware that there was such a thing. But from what the guard said, all he knows is that it is a book about the Savior he knows and loves.

He carefully opens its sacred pages for the first time in his life, and for the next few days he drinks in its truths about Jesus of Nazareth. Does his faith stand or fall on the New Testament truths? No. His faith was strong before he even opened the Scriptures. However, his faith is now *strengthened* by the fact that this 2,000-year-old book *confirmed his experience*. It brought him comfort.[116] It explained why he suddenly longed for Christian fellowship.[117] It mentioned his peace that passed all understanding,[118] and it spoke about why he loved Jesus Christ (whom he had never seen), and why he had an unspeakable joy that bubbled within him.[119] It addressed the fact that he was born again,[120] was a new creature in Christ,[121] and why he continually thought of Jesus of Nazareth[122] and the cross.[123]

This was the experience of the converted at the birth of Christianity. Early Christians didn't have a Bible. It wasn't yet compiled. Most couldn't read. Besides, there was no such thing as the printing press. They were saved by believing the spoken message that they heard.

How do I know that Christianity is true? Is it dependent on the inspiration of the Bible? No. My faith doesn't rise or fall on that fact. Remember, I can be a Christian and not even know that the Bible exists. The Scriptures simply confirm my experience and provide spiritual nourishment to help me to grow in my faith.[124] Christianity isn't true because the Bible confirms it. It is true with or without the Scriptures.

I believe in Jesus Christ because I know Him experientially. The moral Law put me at the edge of a plane door, looking in horror at a 10,000-foot drop. The gospel perfectly ad dressed that problem. I am persuaded of the absolute truth of Christianity because it answered my need for a Savior and made me a new person in Jesus Christ.

Dwight Eisenhower rightly surmised,

It takes no brains to be an atheist. Any stupid person can deny the existence of a supernatural power because man's physical senses cannot detect it. But there cannot be ignored the influence of conscience, the respect we feel for the moral Law, the mystery of first life ... or the marvelous order in which the universe moves about us on this earth. All these evidence the handiwork of the beneficent Deity ... That

Deity is the God of the Bible and Jesus Christ, His Son.

Test It for Yourself

For anyone who is open to the truth, there is indeed 100 percent scientific (knowledge-producing) proof of God:

- **Creation** produces *intellectual knowledge* of God.

    For since the creation of the world His invisible at tributes are clearly seen, being understood by the things that are made, even His eternal power and God head, so that they are without excuse. (Romans 1:20)

- **Conscience** produces *subconscious knowledge* of God.

    ...who show the work of the law written in their hearts, their conscience also bearing witness, and between themselves their thoughts accusing or else excusing them. (Romans 2:15)

- **Conversion** produces *experiential knowledge* of God.

    Jesus said, "He who has My commandments and keeps them, it is he who loves Me. And he who loves Me will be loved by My Father, and I will love him and manifest Myself to him." (John 14:21)

Creation reveals that there is an omnipotent, divine Creator to whom we owe our existence.

It leaves us without excuse for chopping down a tree and carving an idol, and then falling before that idol and believing it is the Creator ... or believing that "Mother Nature" is all there is.

It is the human *conscience* that points to the moral character and the requirements of God. We know that if there is a universal moral Law, then there is a Lawgiver—a God to whom we are accountable. It is the Law of God that awakens the conscience so that we can hear its voice of alarm, and turn in repentance and faith to the only Savior, Jesus Christ.

God has revealed Himself to us in the physical world and in our conscience. There's one way to prove to yourself that God exists. Flick the switch.

ALLEGED MISTAKES IN THE BIBLE

"It's not the parts of the Bible I don't understand that bother me, it's the parts I do understand."

—Mark Twain

As mentioned earlier, many people who reject Christianity do so because they believe the Bible is full of errors. Yet they've never taken the time to actually read it through. After reading the Bible every day without fail for thirty-five years, I have found that any "mistakes" I've seen in the Bible were my mistakes. But there are many seeming contradictions. Let me give you an example. God, through one of the prophets, told a king named Zedekiah that he would be taken captive to Jerusalem. Another prophecy said that he would *not* see Jerusalem. So there's an obvious "mistake" in the Bible. How could he be taken captive to Jerusalem and yet not see it?

The Scriptures tell us that the king was taken captive by Nebuchadnezzar to the main gates of Jerusalem, where he was blinded by his captors (see 2 Kings 23:7). So he was taken captive to Jerusalem, but he didn't see it.

In another seeming contradiction, the four Gospels give four differing accounts as to what was written on the sign that hung on the cross. Matthew said, "This is Jesus the King of the Jews" (27:37). However, Mark contradicts that with "The King of the Jews" (15:26). Luke says something different: "This is the King of the Jews" (23:38), and John maintains that the sign read "Jesus of Nazareth, the King of the Jews" (19:19). Those who are looking for contradictions may therefore say, "See—the Bible is full of mistakes!" and choose to reject it entirely as being untrustworthy. However, those who trust God have no problem harmonizing the Gospels. There is no contradiction if the sign simply read "This is Jesus of Nazareth, the King of the Jews."

The godly base their confidence on two truths: 1) "All Scripture is given by inspiration of God" (2 Timothy 3:16); and 2) an elementary rule of Scripture is that God has deliberately included seeming contradictions in His Word to "snare" the proud. He has "hidden" things from the "wise and prudent" and "revealed them to babes" (Luke 10:21), purposely choosing foolish things to confound the wise (1 Corinthians 1:27). If an ungodly man refuses to humble himself and obey the gospel, and instead desires to build a case against the Bible, God gives him enough material to build his own gallows.

Another seeming mistake is where Adam was told that he would surely die "the day" he ate the fruit of the tree of the knowledge of good and evil. Skeptics point to the Scriptures saying that Adam lived until he was over 900 years old. Here is another obvious "mistake"—for those who don't understand the nature of man. God created mankind with three main parts: body, soul, and spirit (see I Thessalonians 5:23). The body is the machine we walk around in, and our five senses enable us to be conscious of our surroundings. Our soul is our self-conscious part—the area of the emotions, the will, and the conscience. And our spirit is our God-conscious part. That's how we can be aware of God and relate to Him.

We have physical life when we're joined to our body, and we have spiritual life when we're joined to God. Just as physical death occurs when we're separated from our body, spiritual death occurs when we're separated from God. The fact that so-called atheists and agnostics exist attests to the fact that their God-consciousness is dead. They know God exists intellectually—because of conscience and creation—but they are not *aware* of His omnipresence because they are dead spiritually. They are like a fish in the ocean that is not aware of the ocean.

Adam was unique in that when he was created, God breathed His Spirit into him, giving

Adam spiritual life—so he could know and relate to His Creator.

The truth is that Adam *did* die on the day he sinned against God through disobedience. Because God is so holy that He cannot dwell with sin, He withdrew His Holy Spirit from Adam when he sinned, and Adam died *spiritually* at that very moment. And since everything reproduces "after its own kind," all of Adam's offspring (all mankind) are also born spiritually dead—separated from God. The Bible says that we are "dead in trespasses and sins" until we are born again and the life of God enters us through the Holy Spirit. When we repent of our sins and trust in Jesus Christ, the Bible tells us that we "pass from death to life" (John 5:24).

Lot's Stupidity

The following are additional verses cited by atheists as further proof that the Bible cannot be trusted:

> If two men fight together, and the wife of one draws near to rescue her husband from the hand of the one attacking him, and puts out her hand and seizes him by the genitals, then you shall cut off her hand; your eye shall not pity her. (Deuteronomy 25:11,12)

There is no case recorded in Scripture of this ever taking place. However, Jesus said in Matthew 5:30 that if our hand causes us to sin, we should cut it off and cast it from us. This doesn't mean that we should literally cut our hands off. It merely shows us the serious nature of sinning against God.

Some skeptics also point to Genesis 19:8, where a man named Lot offered two of his daughters to a pack of homosexuals who were at his door, threatening to rape Lot's two male visitors:

> "See now, I have two daughters who have not known a man; please, let me bring them out to you, and you may do to them as you wish; only do nothing to these men, since this is the reason they have come under the shadow of my roof."

Of course, the homosexuals didn't take him up on his offer, and the visitors (angels) were very capable of protecting themselves. The Bible doesn't hide human stupidly; it reveals it so that we won't make the same mistakes. We are told that all of Scripture was written for our instruction. So, be instructed. If rapists come to your door, don't offer them your daughters. That's crazy.

Skeptics also mockingly point to the food laws in the Book of Leviticus:

> But all in the seas or in the rivers that do not have fins and scales, all that move in the water or any living thing which is in the water, they are an abomination to you. They shall be an abomination to you; you shall not eat their flesh, but you shall regard

their carcasses as an abomination. (Leviticus 11:10,11)

While there were undoubtedly some health issues involved with eating the scavengers (trash collectors) of the sea, God's primary purpose was for Israel to be a distinct people, separated from the customs of their idolatrous neighbors. This is also the reason they were prohibited from wearing garments made with wool and linen woven together (Deuteronomy 22:11), which was a superstitious custom of the pagans. Many similar regulations were symbolic to keep Israel pure and unmixed with the surrounding nations.

> *The only way he will ever appreciate the beauty and harmony of the painting is to step back and see the whole picture. The same is true of Scripture.*

The Bible can appear to be confusing or contradictory—especially when a verse is pulled out of context. But when something doesn't make sense to me, as a Christian I have the choice to doubt or to trust. Based on my knowledge of God's ability and His integrity, I have chosen the latter.

A Nearsighted View

The professed atheist looks at the Scriptures the same way an extremely nearsighted man would look at the Mona Lisa. To him, the painting is nothing but a meaningless blur, so he approaches it and studies it from a distance of one inch (the only distance at which he can see anything in focus). Then he steps back and writes a review of the work.

Naturally, the review is a horrible one. This is because the only way he will ever appreciate the beauty and harmony of the painting is to step back and see the whole picture. The same is true of Scripture. The Bible is intended to be read as a whole; when the complete picture is seen, it makes perfect sense.

The following are examples of alleged contradictions and mistakes in the Bible, sent to me by Todd Allen Gates, author of *Dialogue with a Christian Proselytizer*. Todd is a friend who is not presently a Christian, yet he very kindly sends me the atheist perspective on certain issues.[125]

In these examples, the atheist compiler takes two seemingly contradictory Bible verses and puts them beside each other to try to prove that the Bible is filled with mistakes. So let's look at the Bible through the eyes of the spiritually nearsighted and see how he sees things. (Note that the wording below is not the actual text given in Scripture, but is the individual's understanding of the verses.)

1) God is omnipotent. Nothing is impossible for God. (Gene sis 17:1; 35:11; 1 Chronicles 29:11,12; Luke 1:37)

Although God was with Judah, together they could not defeat the plainsmen, because the plainsmen had iron chariots. (Judges 1:19)

The assumption is that because God was with Judah, they were therefore promised victory over their enemies. This is clearly a faulty deduction. It is true that nothing is impossible with God and that He was with Judah, but the problem was their disobedience. Even though they had earlier been assured of victory against their enemies with iron chariots (Joshua 17:18), they apparently became fearful and failed to trust God to give them victory. God is with the believer; nothing is impossible for Him to accomplish through those who obey Him. There is no contradiction.

2) Happy is the man who finds wisdom. Get wisdom: it is a beautiful crown upon your head. (Proverbs 3:13; 4:7–10; 19:8)

Wisdom is foolishness. (I Corinthians 1:19–21; 3:19–20)

The verses from the Book of Proverbs are speaking of the precious wisdom that comes from God. The two New Testament passages are comparing the wisdom of God specifically with the foolish "wisdom of this world" (epitomized by atheism). No contradiction.

3) Sacrifices can, in at least some cases, take away sin. (Numbers 15:24–28)

Sacrifices can never take away sin. (Hebrews 10:11)

Once again, to make sense of the whole picture of what the Bible is saying, one has to stand back a little and focus. We are told in Scripture that the Old Testament sacrifices could never make the person offering them "perfect." Each time Israel sinned, they would have to make further atonement (see Hebrews 9:9). However, when God provided His own sacrificial Lamb (Jesus of Nazareth), Jesus' death on the cross accomplished what the sacrificial system could not do. It made the believer perfect in the sight of God. Here are those verses in context (speaking of the Messiah):

> Then He said, "Behold, I have come to do Your will, O God." He takes away the first that He may establish the second. By that will we have been sanctified through the offering of the body of Jesus Christ once for all. And every priest stands ministering daily and offering repeatedly the same sacrifices, which can never take away sins. But this Man, after He had offered one sacrifice for sins forever, sat down at the right hand of God, from that time waiting till His enemies are made His footstool. For by one offering He has perfected forever those who are being sanctified. (Hebrews 10:9–14)

The Numbers passage does not say that sacrifices can "take away sin," just that God offered temporary forgiveness through the sacrificial system. Humanity's sin debt wasn't "paid in full" until Jesus shed His blood in payment. It's like the difference between accepting a check as payment, and actually cashing the check and receiving the funds. There is no contradiction.

4) No work is to be done on the Sabbath, not even lighting a fire. The commandment is permanent, and death is required for infractions. (Exodus 20:8–11; 31:15–17; 35:1–3)

Paul says the Sabbath commandment was temporary, and to decide for yourself regarding its observance. (Romans 14:5; Colossians 2:14–16)

Scripture makes it clear that no one can be justified (made right with God) by keeping the Sabbath holy, or by keeping any other Commandment. The way we are made right with God is by grace, through faith in Jesus Christ (see Ephesians 2:8,9).

Jesus fulfilled the demands of the Law, which means that you and I can be made right with God through faith in Him alone. Believers now serve in the spirit, not the letter of the law, and the principle behind the Sabbath is this: Just as God created for six days then rested on the seventh, man is to work for six days and rest on the seventh—to cease working. Those who trust in Christ's finished work on the cross have ceased trying to be justified through their own efforts and instead find their rest in Him. (See Hebrews 4:3,10.) That's why the keeping of the Sabbath is a non-issue for Christians when it comes to eternal salvation. So, the issue boils down to a matter of the conscience. Christians have incredible liberty—no one can tell us what we must eat or drink, or what days we must observe. Here is the context of Colossians 2:14-16:

> ...having wiped out the handwriting of requirements that was against us, which was contrary to us. And He has taken it out of the way, having nailed it to the cross. Having disarmed principalities and powers, He made a public spectacle of them, triumphing over them in it. So let no one judge you in food or in drink, or regarding a festival or a new moon or sabbaths.

It makes sense that anyone who doesn't understand why Christ died would end up confused about the Scriptures. The Law was never meant to justify anyone; all it does is bring the knowledge of sin to show us that we need a Savior. There is no contradiction between the verses.

5) Love your enemies. Love your neighbor as yourself. (Matthew 5:43,44; 22:39)

Go nowhere among the Gentiles nor enter a Samaritan town. (Matthew 10:5)

The atheist infers that, because Jesus told His disciples to "love your enemies" and to "love your neighbor" but then told them not to go to certain groups of people, this proves He didn't love the Gentiles or the Samaritans.

However, the plan of God was to preach the gospel to the Jews first before taking it to the Gentiles. This wasn't because of a lack of love and concern for them, but because the Jews already had the Law which prepared them for the message of grace. No contradiction.

6) The covenant of circumcision is to be everlasting. (Genesis 17:7,10–11)

> Circumcision is of no consequence. (Galatians 6:15)

The means by which a man is justified in the sight of God isn't through circumcision or any external observance, but only through faith in Jesus Christ. If you read the Galatians verse in context, in verse 12 Paul points out that "not even those who are circumcised keep the law." The outward symbolism is worthless for their salvation if their heart is not right with God, as he explains in Romans 2:28,29:

> For he is not a Jew who is one outwardly, nor is circumcision that which is outward in the flesh; but he is a Jew who is one inwardly; and circumcision is that of the heart, in the Spirit, not in the letter; whose praise is not from men but from God.

The "circumcision" that God desires is that of the heart, which occurs when a person is born again and receives a new heart and new spirit. That's why Paul writes, "For in Christ Jesus neither circumcision nor uncircumcision avails anything, but a new creation" (Galatians 6:15). Again, there is no contradiction.

7) It is wrong to lend money at interest. (Leviticus 25:37)

It is right to lend money at interest. (Matthew 25:27; Luke 19:23–27)

Here is the context of Leviticus 25:37 (notice that the Bible is speaking of lending money to fellow Jews—"your brother"):

> If one of your brethren becomes poor, and falls into poverty among you, then you shall help him, like a stranger or a sojourner, that he may live with you. Take no usury or interest from him; but fear your God, that your brother may live with you. You shall not lend him your money for usury, nor lend him your food at a profit. (Leviticus 25:35–37)

In the New Testament passages, Jesus is not speaking in the context of Jews lending Jewish brothers money. These passages don't even specifically mention lending of money; the profit could be earned by buying and selling goods. Besides, these are parables in which Jesus was teaching a *spiritual* principle; He's not advising that people be slain for not investing (Matthew 25:30; Luke 19:27). No contradiction.

8) A castrate may not enter the assembly of the Lord. (Deuteronomy 23:1)

Men are encouraged to consider making themselves castrates for the sake of the Kingdom of God. (Matthew 19:12)

In ancient times, some parents in the East would mutilate their children with the intent of training them for service in the houses of the great. (As eunuchs they would be more trustworthy as personal servants.) The instruction in Deuteronomy is intended to discourage this practice.

For comparison, here is Matthew 19:12 in context:

> [Jesus'] disciples said to Him, "If such is the case of the man with his wife, it is better not to marry." He said to them, "All cannot accept this saying, but only those to whom it has been given: For there are eunuchs who were born thus from their mother's womb, and there are eunuchs who were made eunuchs by men, and there are eunuchs who have made themselves eunuchs for the kingdom of heaven's sake. He who is able to accept it, let him accept it." (Matthew 19:10–12)

It is quite a stretch to say that "men are *encouraged* to consider making themselves castrates." Jesus' latter statement is referring to those who are practical "eunuchs" by remaining abstinent. Jesus is not encouraging the practice of castration, but is explaining why few can accept a lifestyle of celibacy. There is no contraction between these two verses.

9) Do not rejoice when your enemy falls or stumbles. (Proverbs 24:16–18)

The righteous shall rejoice when he sees vengeance. (Psalm 58:10,11)

The context of Psalm 58:10,11 is God's judgment of the wicked:

The righteous shall rejoice when he sees the vengeance; he shall wash his feet in the blood of the wicked, so that men will say, "Surely there is a reward for the righteous; surely He is God who judges in the earth."

There is a big difference between rejoicing when misfortune comes and when justice is eventually done. No contradiction.

10) Jesus did not come to abolish the law. (Matthew 5:17–19; Luke 16:17)

Jesus did abolish the law. (Ephesians 2:13–15; Hebrews 7:18,19)

Once again, it would seem that the atheist has no understanding as to the reason Christ suffered and died. He came to fulfill the Law so that those who trust in Him could be justified (pronounced not guilty and made clean in the sight of God).

Think of two brothers who both have large court fines. They don't have any money and are about to be sentenced to prison terms. Their kindly father loves them and pays their fines. He satisfies the demands of the law by fulfilling the court's requirements. Both men are then free to go. However, one of them refuses to accept the payment. He is therefore still under the law's penalty, and he is sentenced to a long prison term. He was thrown in prison even though the father satisfied the law's demand through his payment.

Jesus didn't come to do away with the moral Law. It is eternal and will be the standard of judgment on Judgment Day. He came to satisfy its demands for those who trust Him—making provision for our forgiveness by paying our fine in His life's blood.

Here is Matthew 5:17,18:

> "Do not think that I came to destroy the Law or the Prophets. I did not come to destroy but to fulfill. For assuredly, I say to you, till heaven and earth pass away, one jot or one tittle will by no means pass from the law till all is fulfilled."

Here is Ephesians 2:13–15:

> But now in Christ Jesus you who once were far off have been brought near by the blood of Christ. For He Himself is our peace, who has made both one, and has broken down the middle wall of separation, having abolished in His flesh the enmity, that is, the law of commandments contained in ordinances, so as to create in Himself one new man from the two, thus making peace.

Christians (both Jew and Gentile) are no longer under the wrath of the Law, because they trust in Jesus Christ. However, those who are outside of Christ (refusing His blood payment) are still under its wrath (see John 3:36). No contradiction.

11) God's anger does not last forever. (Psalm 30:5; Jeremiah 3:12; Micah 7:18)

God's anger lasts forever. (Jeremiah 17:4; Matthew 25:46)

There are two types of God's anger mentioned in these verses. The first is a reference to His temporal anger against sin. Because He is merciful, He forgives those who turn to Him in true repentance. For example, here is Jeremiah 3:12 in context:

> Then the LORD said to me, "Backsliding Israel has shown herself more righteous than treacherous Judah. Go and proclaim these words toward the north, and say: 'Return, backsliding Israel,' says the LORD; 'I will not cause My anger to fall on you. For I am merciful,' says the LORD; 'I will not remain angry forever. That you have transgressed against the LORD your God, and have scattered your charms to alien deities under every green tree, and you have not obeyed My voice,' says the LORD." (Jeremiah 3:11–13)

God is speaking to sinful Israel. However, Matthew 25:46 is a fearful reference to those who are the damned—those who die in their sins. One is a temporal anger, the other is eternal. There is no contradiction.

12) The earth was established forever. (Psalm 78:69; Ecclesiastes 1:4; 3:14)

The earth will someday perish. (Psalm 102:25,26; Matthew 24:35; Mark 13:31; Luke 21:33; Hebrews 1:10,11; 2 Peter 3:10)

God has established that the earth will exist forever, though it will be completely remade. At the end of time He is going to make a new heavens and a new earth (see Isaiah 65:17; 2 Peter 3:13), and will make all things new to remove the curse of sin (see Revelation 21:1). Once again, there is no contradiction.

As you can see from these few samples, stepping back to consider *all* of Scripture paints an entirely different picture than when examining two random verses.

What a tragedy it is when atheists "twist Scripture to their own destruction," and it is an even greater tragedy when people read their writings and embrace them as the gospel truth. Many do this without even having read the Bible for themselves. If you will take the time to consider the Bible as a whole, you will be able to comprehend its flawless beauty and amazing harmony, and will see that it is indeed the inspired words of our Creator—God's revelation of Himself to man.

12

COMMON OBJECTIONS TO CHRISTIANITY

"I seem to have been only a boy playing on the sea-shore, and diverting myself in now and then finding a smoother pebble or a prettier shell than ordinary, whilst the great ocean of truth lay all undiscovered before me."

—Isaac Newton

The dictionary gives numerous meanings for the word "lost." One definition is "having gone astray or missed the way; bewildered as to place, direction, etc." There is one thing worse than being lost. It is being lost and not knowing it. Perhaps that describes you. Let's find out by asking you three searching questions. The first is, Do you know the origin of the species of which you are a part? If you don't accept the Genesis explanation for our origins, the odds are you haven't any idea where humans came from.

The second question is, What is the purpose of human existence? Why are you here? If you don't accept the biblical explanation for mankind's purpose (that we are created by God, for God), then you will have no idea why you are here. Third question: Where are you going? In other words, what happens after death? More than likely you will be confined to the arena of speculation. You don't know what eternity holds for you. The best you have is a guess—a stab in the dark. So there you have it. You don't know where you came from, you don't know what you are doing here, and you don't know where you are going. You are "lost." As the Bible says, you are like a sheep that has gone astray, and the Scriptures tell us that the Good Shepherd came "to seek and save that which was lost."

Years ago a small child disappeared in the outback of Australia. His parents and searchers frantically looked for him for days. Finally, the frightened, hungry child emerged from the dense bush, because he saw his father. His first words were, "Dad, I've been looking for you!" It turned out that he had been hiding from those he believed were his enemies. From his perspective, the bush was filled with big people who were yelling his name and hitting the shrubs with sticks. So he hid from them.

Maybe that's what you have been doing. You have been hiding from your searchers. You have hidden in the bushes of excuse and what you see as reason and logic. Perhaps there are certain questions that are between you and your coming out in the open with God. So I ask you the same question the apostle Paul asked his hearers:

"Have I therefore become your enemy because I tell you the truth?" God is searching for you. He is calling your name. As a follower of Jesus, I too am compelled to seek and save the lost. I know that if you stay in hiding you will have a terrible fate. I have no other agenda but to see you found by God and saved from His wrath. So, let's try to address some of the questions you may have been asking. (These were taken from *The Evidence Bible*, where you can find answers to one hundred of the most commonly asked questions about the Christian faith.)

"What about suffering—doesn't that prove there isn't a loving God?"

Study the soil for a moment. It naturally produces weeds. No one plants them; no one waters them. They even stubbornly push through cracks of a dry sidewalk. Millions of useless weeds sprout like there's no tomorrow, strangling our crops and ruining our lawns. Pull them out by the roots, and there will be more the following day. They are nothing but a curse!

Consider how much of the earth is uninhabitable. There are millions of square miles of barren deserts in Africa and other parts of the world. Most of Australia is nothing but miles and miles of useless desolate land. Not only that, but the earth is constantly shaken with massive earthquakes. Its shores are lashed with hurricanes; tornadoes rip through creation with incredible fury; devastating floods soak the land; and terrible droughts parch the soil.

> *Did God blow it when He created humanity? What sort of tyrant must our Creator be if this was His master plan?*

Sharks, tigers, lions, snakes, spiders, and disease-carrying mosquitoes attack humanity and suck its life's blood. The earth's inhabitants are afflicted with disease, pain, suffering, and death. Think of how many people are plagued with cancer, Alzheimer's, multiple sclerosis, heart disease, emphysema, Parkinson's, and a number of other debilitating illnesses. Consider all the children with leukemia, or people born with crippling diseases or without the mental capability to even feed themselves. All these things should convince thinking minds that something is radically wrong.

Did God blow it when He created humanity? What sort of tyrant must our Creator be if this was His master plan? Sadly, many use the issue of suffering as an excuse to reject any thought of God, when its existence is the very reason we should believe Him. Suffering stands as terrible testimony to the truth of the explanation given by the Word of God. But how can we know that the Bible is true? Simply by studying the prophecies of Matthew 24, Luke 21, and 2 Timothy 3. A few minutes of openhearted inspection will convince any honest skeptic that this is no ordinary book. It is the supernatural testament of our Creator about why there is suffering ... and what we can do about it.

The Bible tells us that God cursed the earth because of Adam's transgression. Weeds are a curse. So is disease. Sin and suffering cannot be separated. The Scriptures inform us that we live in a fallen creation. In the beginning, God created man perfect, and he lived in a perfect world without suffering. It was heaven on earth. When sin came into the world, death and misery came with it. Those who understand the message of Holy Scripture eagerly await a new heaven and a new earth "in which righteousness dwells." In that coming Kingdom there will be no more pain, suffering, disease, or death. We are told that no eye has ever seen, nor has any ear heard, neither has any man's mind ever imagined the wonderful things that God has in store for those who love Him (1 Corinthians 2:9). Think for a moment what it would be like if food grew with the fervor of weeds. Consider how wonderful it would be if the deserts became incredibly fertile, if creation stopped devouring humanity. Imagine if the weather worked for us instead of against us, if disease completely disappeared, if pain was a thing of the past, if death was no more.

The dilemma is that we are like a child whose insatiable appetite for chocolate has caused his face to break out with ugly sores. He looks in the mirror and sees a sight that makes him depressed. But instead of giving up his beloved chocolate, he consoles himself by stuffing more into his mouth. Yet, the source of his pleasure is actually the cause of his suffering. The whole face of the earth is nothing but ugly sores of suffering. Everywhere we look we see unspeakable pain. But instead of believing God's explanation and asking Him to forgive us and change our appetite, we run deeper into sin's sweet embrace. There we find solace in its temporal pleasures, thus intensifying our pain, both in this life and in the life to come.

"How can you love God when the Bible encourages the cruelty of slavery?"

The Bible does acknowledge the reality of slavery. But it's important to realize that we view the subject through the lenses of American slavery, with its incredible cruelty. To be a slave in Bible times was more like being a modern-day servant. In fact the Bible uses the word "bondservant" when referring to slaves. The apostle Paul, in the New Testament, speaks of being a "slave" of Jesus Christ.

There is provision for whipping of a slave who violates the Law, but it's important to note that the harshness of the Law wasn't confined to slaves. It was for all of Israel. The Law dealt out the death sentence for adultery, blasphemy, rape, homosexuality, murder, and rebellion. However, there is no incident recorded in the New Testament of a slave being whipped, or of any rapist, homosexual, or rebellious youth being stoned. People tend to obey the law when it has a bite to it. Not so in modern America, where a murderer can get free food, lodging, cable TV, and gym facilities for 6 to 10 years, and perhaps end up being freely taught a trade. No wonder 200,000 murders took place in the U.S. just during the 1990s.

"The Bible says that children were to be stoned to death."

It actually says that if a *youth* was a continual drunkard and was rebellious, his parents had the option to take him to the elders and have him stoned to death. Again, there is no record in Scripture of that happening. This was no doubt because each child was told what the Law warned would happen to him if he transgressed its precepts. However, hundreds of thousands of young people in this country have died simply because they gave themselves to illicit drugs, alcohol, and rebellion.

"What kind of God would tell Joshua to kill the Canaanites—every man, woman, and child?"

Let me tell you about my father. When I was young, he continually left my mom and us three kids to fend for ourselves. And I was there when he killed a helpless animal with his bare hands. If that was entirely the case, you could be justified in believing that my father was a tyrant. However, there's some missing information. The reason he left us each day was to work to earn money to provide food, clothing, and shelter for us. And the reason he killed a helpless animal was because it had been hit by a car and was in agony. He put it out of its misery, and it grieved him to do so.

So, now you can have a balanced view of my dad. He was a loving father and a very compassionate man.

One view of God from the Bible can paint Him to be a tyrant, but in the entirety of Scripture we see a different picture. God bestowed life on each of us. Think of what He did for you. He gave you life itself, eyes to see with, ears to hear beautiful music, and taste buds to enjoy delicious food. He created the blueness of the sky and the awe of a sunset. He gave you a nose to smell the fragrance of flowers. He lavished you with His kindness. He didn't treat you according to your sins, but has shown incredible mercy to you in allowing you to live this far. Add to that the fact that He became a person in Jesus Christ, and in Him we see the most compassionate, loving person who ever lived. He demonstrated His love for us by suffering unspeakably and dying for our sins.

With that extra knowledge, it's easy for me to look at anything God did and say, "All His judgments are righteous and true altogether." You say, "But he instigated the deaths of men, women, and children!" Yes, and He did that not just with the Canaanites, but with the whole of humanity. The Judge of the universe said, "The soul that sins shall die" (Ezekiel 18:20). God proclaimed the death sentence on every man, woman, and child. But this same God of justice is rich in mercy and will grant everlasting life to every man, woman, and child who will humble themselves, repent of their sin, and trust in Jesus Christ.

"Religion has caused more wars than anything else in history."

Not quite. When it comes to committing atrocities, religion comes in second. Atheistic communism comes in at number one. It's caused the death of more than one hundred million people.

But it is true that millions have been oppressed and murdered because man has used religion for political gain. Jesus tells us in John 16:2,3 that there will be some who, in their error, commit atrocities and murder in the name of God: "The time is coming that whoever kills you will think that he offers God service." However, He informs us that these are not true believers: "And these things they will do to you because they have not known the Father nor Me." The Bible also tells us that "no murderer has eternal life abiding in him" (1 John 3:15).

Jesus told His followers to love their enemies. So if a man puts a knife into someone's back in the name of Christianity, something obviously isn't right. If we human beings can detect it, how much more will God? He will deal with it on Judgment Day.

"Hitler was a Christian!"

Despite the fact that Adolf Hitler had a Roman Catholic background, he became adamantly anti-Christian and believed in evolution. We can find definitive proof of his real views in the following quotes by Hitler, taken from *Hitler's Table Talk* (London: Weidenfeld & Nicholson, 1953):

> National Socialism and religion cannot exist together ... The heaviest blow that

ever struck humanity was the coming of Christianity. Bolshevism is Christianity's illegitimate child. Both are inventions of the Jew. The deliberate lie in the matter of religion was introduced into the world by Christianity ... Let it not be said that Christianity brought man the life of the soul, for that evolution was in the natural order of things. (pp.6–7)

The reason why the ancient world was so pure, light and serene was that it knew nothing of the two great scourges: the pox and Christianity. (p.75)

Christianity is an invention of sick brains: one could imagine nothing more senseless, nor any more indecent way of turning the idea of the Godhead into a mockery ... When all is said, we have no reason to wish that the Italians and Spaniards should free themselves from the drug of Christianity. Let's be the only people who are immunized against the disease. (pp.118–119)

There is something very unhealthy about Christianity. (p.339)

It would always be disagreeable for me to go down to posterity as a man who made concessions in this field. I realize that man, in his imperfection, can commit innumerable errors—but to devote myself deliberately to errors, that is something I cannot do. I shall never come personally to terms with the Christian lie. Our epoch in the next 200 years will certainly see the end of the disease of Christianity ... My regret will have been that I couldn't ... behold [its demise]. (p.278)

"What about Galileo—didn't the Church persecute him?"

Galileo had the audacity to question what science of his day believed—something called "geocentricity," the belief that the Earth is the center of the universe and the sun revolves around it. The Roman Catholic church condemned Galileo in the 17th century for supporting Nicolaus Copernicus' discovery that the Earth revolved around the sun. According to *Great Lives, Great Deeds*, "Galileo was summoned to Rome [where] he was threatened with torture unless he recanted his scientific views. After four months in detention he yielded abjectly to the Vatican."[126] His scientific beliefs didn't contradict the Scriptures, but they contradicted the teaching of the Catholic church and the science of the day.

"The church is full of hypocrites."

Hypocrites may show up at a church building every Sunday, but there are no hypocrites in the Church (Christ's body). *Hypocrite* comes from the Greek word for "actor," or pretender. Hypocrisy is "the practice of professing beliefs, feelings, or virtues that one does not hold." The Church is made up of true believers; hypocrites are "pretenders" who sit among God's people.

I don't blame anyone for rejecting "religion" based on this hypocrisy. On one hand we have a religion that is filled with pedophiles and on the other money-grabbing evangelists. If I was the treasurer of the Catholic or Protestant church for ten minutes, I would write out checks so fast to feed the hungry, clothe the poor, and promote the gospel that flames would leap off the paper. There are more actors in the church than there are in Hollywood. Hypocrisy runs rampant in the modern church—but be careful if you judge it. Look at this warning from the Bible:

> *There are more actors in the church than there are in Hollywood. Hypocrisy runs rampant in the modern church.*

> Therefore you are inexcusable, O man, whoever you are who judge, for in whatever you judge another you condemn yourself; for you who judge practice the same things. But we know that the judgment of God is according to truth against those who practice such things. And do you think this, O man, you who judge those practicing such

things, and doing the same, that you will escape the judgment of God? Or do you despise the riches of His goodness, forbearance, and longsuffering, not knowing that the goodness of God leads you to repentance? (Romans 2:1–4)

God knows those who love Him, and the Bible warns that He will sort out the true converts from the false on the Day of Judgment. All hypocrites will end up in Hell (Matthew 24:51).

"Who made God?"

The fact of the existence of the Creator is axiomatic (self-evident). That's why the Bible says, "The fool has said in his heart, 'There is no God'" (Psalm 14:1). Some who think that the question "Who made God?" can't be answered feel justified in denying that God exists.

But the question of who made God can be answered by simply looking at space and asking, "Does space have an end?" Obviously, it doesn't. If there is a brick wall with "The End" written on it, the question arises, "What is behind the brick wall?" Strain the mind though it may, we have to believe (have faith) that space has no beginning and no end. The same applies with God. He has no beginning and no end. He is eternal.

The Bible also informs us that time is a dimension that God created, into which man was subjected:

> [God] who has saved us and called us with a holy calling, not according to our works, but according to His own purpose and grace which was given to us in Christ Jesus *before time began*. (2 Timothy 1:9)
>
> ...in hope of eternal life which God, who cannot lie, promised *before time began*. (Titus 1:2)

It even tells us that one day time will no longer exist. That will be called "eternity." God Himself dwells outside of the dimension He created. He dwells in eternity and is not subject to time. God spoke history before it came into being. He can move through time as a man flips through a history book. Because we live in the dimension of time, logic and reason demand that everything must have a beginning and an end. We can understand the concept of God's eternal nature the same way we understand the concept of space having no beginning and end—by faith. We simply have to believe they are so, even though such thoughts put a strain on our distinctly insufficient cerebrum.

Some atheists claim that if God can be infinite, then the universe can also be without beginning. The illogical presumption here is that "the universe has an intelligence in and of itself," because intelligence is required to carry out the order we call creation. If that is correct, the only logical conclusion would be that the universe somehow has the ability to think and to create from nothing ... but then we would be describing God. So, in essence, atheists are presuming the universe is God. That can only cause us to conclude the obvious: they are quite willing to accept that there is some kind of "God" (creative intelligence), but just don't like the God of the Bible—or any God who has a moral code and condemns those who violate it.

"Didn't men write the Bible?"

When you write a letter, do you write the letter, or does the pen? Obviously you do; the pen is merely the instrument you use. God used men as instruments to write His "letter" to humanity. They ranged from kings to common fishermen, but the 66 books of the Bible were all given by inspiration of God. Evidence that this is no ordinary book can be seen with a quick study of its prophecies, among other things.

"In saying 'an eye for an eye,' the Bible encourages taking the law into our own hands by avenging wrongdoing."

This verse is so often misquoted by the world. Many believe it is giving a license to take matters into our own hands and render evil for evil. In reality, it is referring to civil law concerning restitution. If someone steals your ox, he is to restore the ox. If someone steals and wrecks your car, he is to buy you another one: a car for a car, an eye for an eye, a tooth for a tooth. The spirit of what Jesus is saying here is radically different from the "sue the shirt off the back of your neighbor" society in which we live.

"Jesus Christ never even existed."

Surprisingly, some skeptics claim that Jesus didn't exist, though to do so they have to reject the entire New Testament historical record. The New Testament contains hundreds of references to Jesus Christ, and in terms of ancient manuscript evidence, this is extraordinarily strong proof of the existence of a man named Jesus of Nazareth in the early first century A.D.

While skeptics may choose to reject the Bible's moral message, they cannot deny its historical accuracy. Over 25,000 archaeological finds demonstrate that the people, places, and events mentioned in the Bible are real and are accurately described. No archaeological finding has ever refuted the Bible. In fact, the descriptions in the Bible have often led archaeologists to amazing discoveries. Non-Christian journalist Jeffery Sheler, author of the book *Is the Bible True?*, concluded, "In extraordinary ways, modern archeology is affirming the historical core of the Old and New Testaments, supporting key portions of crucial biblical stories."[127]

In addition, a surprising amount of information about Jesus can be drawn from secular historical sources. Writings confirming His birth, ministry, death, and resurrection include Flavius Josephus (A.D.93), the Babylonian Talmud (A.D.70–200), Pliny the Younger's letter to the Emperor Trajan (approx. A.D.100), the Annals of Tacitus (A.D.115–117), Mara Bar Serapion (sometime after A.D.73), and Suetonius' Life of Claudius and Life of Nero (A.D.120).

The first-century Roman Tacitus, considered one of the more accurate historians of the ancient world, mentioned superstitious "Christians," named after Christus (Latin for Christ), who was executed by Pontius Pilate during the reign of Tiberius. Suetonius, chief secretary to Emperor Hadrian, wrote of a man named Chrestus (Christ) who lived during the first century (Roman Annals 15.44). Renowned Jewish historian Josephus wrote:

> Now, there was about this time Jesus, a wise man [if it be lawful to call him a man], for he was a doer of wonderful works, a teacher of such men as receive the truth with pleasure. He drew over to him both many of the Jews, and many of the Gentiles. [He was the Messiah.] And when Pilate, at the suggestion of the

principal men amongst us, had condemned him to the cross, those that loved him at the first did not forsake him [for he appeared to them alive again at the third day; as the divine prophets had foretold these and ten thousand other wonderful things concerning him]. And the tribe of Christians, so named from him, are not extinct at this date.[128]

"Which 'god' are you talking about: Thor, Zeus, etc.?"

The inference in this question is, "These were mythical gods, and so is yours." Atheists are correct about these gods being myths. Man gravitates toward idolatry (making up false gods) as a moth does to a flame. There are *millions* of false gods (Hinduism alone has 330 million), but there is only one Creator, and that's the God who revealed Himself to Moses and gave us His moral Law. That is the God you and I will have to face on Judgment Day.

Another argument atheists use is that they can't prove that God doesn't exist, just as you and I can't prove that the tooth fairy doesn't exist. This is a demeaning way of equating belief in God with belief in the tooth fairy. It's true that we cannot disprove the existence of either the tooth fairy or God. However, belief in the existence of the tooth fairy is inconsequential.

Belief *in* and therefore obedience *to* God has *eternal* consequences.

13

CONFESSIONS OF A ROCKET SCIENTIST

"Scientific concepts exist only in the minds of men. Behind these concepts lies the reality which is being revealed to us, but only by the grace of God."

—Wernher von Braun

As mentioned earlier, you don't have to be a rocket scientist to see that there is a problem with evolution, but it doesn't hurt. Wernher von Braun is, without a doubt, the world's most famous rocket scientist. His crowning achievement, as head of NASA's Marshall Space Flight Center, was to lead the development of the Saturn V booster rocket that helped land the first men on the Moon in July 1969. In a letter to the California State Board of Education, which was debating the teaching of evolution, he offered his observations on whether "the case for design" was a viable scientific theory:

> One cannot be exposed to the law and order of the universe without concluding that there must be design and purpose behind it all. In the world round us, we can

behold the obvious manifestations of an ordered, structured plan or design ... The better we understand the intricacies of the universe and all it harbors, the more reason we have found to marvel at the inherent design upon which it is based.

While the admission of a design for the universe ultimately raises the question of a Designer (a subject outside of science), the scientific method does not allow us to exclude data which lead to the conclusion that the universe, life and man are based on design. To be forced to believe only one conclusion—that everything in the universe happened by chance—would violate the very objectivity of science itself. Certainly there are those who argue that the universe evolved out of a random process, but what random process could produce the brain of a man or the system or the human eye?

...They [evolutionists] challenge science to prove the existence of God. But must we really light a candle to see the sun?

If we were created by a divine Being, it's reasonable to expect that God would have given mankind evidence of His existence.

Many men who are intelligent and of good faith say they cannot visualize a Designer. Well, can a physicist visualize an electron? The electron is materially inconceivable and yet it is so perfectly known through its effects that we use it to illuminate our cities, guide our airlines through the night skies and take the most accurate measurements. What strange rationale makes some physicists accept the inconceivable electrons as real while refusing to accept the reality of a Designer on the ground that they cannot conceive Him?...

We in NASA were often asked what the real reason was for the amazing string of successes we had with our Apollo flights to the Moon. I think the only honest answer we could give was that we tried to never overlook anything. It is in that same sense of scientific honesty that I endorse the presentation of alternative theories for the origin of the universe, life and man in the science classroom. It would be an error to overlook the possibility that the universe was planned rather than happening by chance.[129]

This brilliant scientist owed the success of his team to the fact that they "never overlook anything." If you are truly interested in scientific evidence, you will likewise need to have enough "scientific honesty" to not overlook the possibility that our intricate, ordered universe has an intelligent Designer.

The hypothesis that there is no God just didn't pan out—the evidence doesn't fit the theory of evolution. So let's honestly examine the hypothesis that there *is* a God. If we *were* created by a divine Being, it would be important for humans to know that. Therefore, it's reasonable to expect that God would have given mankind evidence of His existence:

- If there is a God, He would be able to make His presence known to us.

  And He does, through creation.

- If there is a God, He would be able to reveal His character and His will to us.

  And He does, through the moral Law written on our conscience.

- If there is a God, He would enable us to not just know *about* Him, but *know Him* personally.

  And He does, through our repentance and faith in the Savior, Jesus Christ.

Those who are intellectually honest follow the evidence wherever it leads. This is what Jason W. Pratt did. An aerospace engineer, Pratt was a typical atheist who put his faith in science. As he began to notice certain contradictions of science, though, he set out to honestly seek the truth.

With an open heart, read along as he describes his search, and see if you arrive at the same conclusion. My prayer is that you will.

I was a self-righteous, self-absorbed atheist when I went off to college to study aerospace engineering in 1988. Now, I am not implying that this description applies to all atheists. I can only speak for myself, but if the shoe fits ... In any case, academics came easy and I was the god of my universe. To prove it, I pretty much did whatever I wanted. I knew I was truly a wonderful person and reasoned that if I did not hurt anyone I was doing just fine. Selfish, but wonderful nonetheless and I had plenty of like-minded friends to prove it.

It did not take long before I encountered individuals who called themselves Christians. I knew the type: hypocrites deluded by a ridiculous ancient tome, every one of them. In fact, I had a string of Christian roommates. I would take pleasure in deriding them and finding any reason to ridicule their faith, their God, and the Bible that guided them. I enjoyed playing their intellectual superior until I came across two individuals. One was a fellow engineering student. He had a 4.0 GPA and was clearly a brilliant individual! The other was my engineering advisor, an authority in the field of thermodynamics; and strangely enough, both were Christians! How could these highly intelligent individuals believe in the God of the Bible? I respected their intellect but certainly not their faith. To make matters worse, my advisor had a young earth creation article on his office door. How could a scientist ignore the clear scientific evidence of evolution?!

While at college I came across people of diverse faiths and I did not have any problem with most of them or their religions. Nevertheless, these Christians really got up my nose, although I never had one instigate any line of argumentation with me. All they needed to do was simply mention the fact that they were Christian and I was seeing red. Why was this? What was it about these Christians in particular that drew my anger? I decided it was that book—you know the one I'm talking about—and the fact that anything was going to contradict my "do as I please as long as nobody gets seriously hurt" morality.

Although I had never actually read very much of the Bible I had plenty of arguments against its claims and its validity. I had enough of these people and their silly book so I decided to break out my superior intellectual hammer to destroy it. I began reading the Bible with the sole intent of picking it apart—all right, tearing it apart. Interestingly enough, it was at about this time that I had absorbed enough hard science and mathematics to make a very simple observation, one I could not ignore.

In studying chemistry, physics, calculus, differential equations, electro-optical physics, vector calculus, thermodynamics, fluid dynamics, structural mechanics, statics and dynamics, and mechanical design, I found a sort of commonality shared by all the systems on earth and even the universe! I could only describe this commonality as a sort of thumbprint, and it was very curious.

As a student of science, which I loved dearly, I was even more captivated by engineering, which uses science in much the same way that a plumber uses a pipe wrench or a carpenter uses a hammer and saw. In fact, one of my favorite quotes was by Theodore von Karman, a Hungarian immigrant who is famous for his work in aerodynamics and aeronautics and co-founded NASA's Jet Propulsion Laboratory. He said, "A scientist discovers that which exists. An engineer creates that which never was."

The concept conveyed in that quote certainly appealed to my own "god complex." I truly became a student of engineering design; it was my first love. So, believe me when I say I can recognize a good design when I see one. As mentioned, I began to notice in the most complex inner workings of every system a common thread of apparent design. For example, some of the functional attributes of various systems—whether electrical, fluid dynamic, or aerodynamic—could be described and researched using the same differential mathematic equation. The mathematical description derived from this equation can be applied to synapses of the human nervous system, the movement (or lack of, if you are in L.A.) of traffic in a transportation system, water flow in an irrigation system, or the behavior of electric current in a computer circuit board. I could go on, but I think you get the point.

My point can be further demonstrated by a brief review of the works of Swiss mathematician Leonhard Euler or my buddy von Karman previously quoted. A quick Internet search of these men will turn up an incredible diversity of their accomplishments across a range of scientific and mathematical fields. What accounts for this breadth in their work? These men noticed a string of commonality that crosses and links various fields of study. They could observe a clear design and (not to trivialize their work) they "simply" set out studying that design to reveal its mysteries and derive mathematical formulas that were equally applicable in the design of an aircraft wing or of the air conditioner in your home.

Let me make one last point regarding true, testable, and verifiable science. In my study of physics and thermodynamics, I began to take notice of something disturbing. As any elementary student of science will tell you, a scientific theory is by definition always subject to the laws of science—always. The principle laws of physics and thermodynamics state a few very basic yet incredible concepts. Newton's first law states that the inertia or momentum of a system is maintained unless acted upon by an outside force. A spinning top demonstrates this concept, as it slows down due to the outside force of friction but it never instantly stops and changes direction. The first law of thermodynamics states that matter and energy can be neither created nor destroyed. Something does not appear out of nothing, and even the explosion of a bomb takes existing matter and energy and changes it into another form of matter and energy but does not categorically destroy either.

The second law of thermodynamics states that the energy of a system is always being reduced to a lower form of energy plus a useless form of energy called entropy or the disorganization of a system. Look at a teenager's room to see what I mean here. It takes a lot of energy to get that room clean but the deterioration of that clean room begins immediately and progresses to a complete mess as the effects of entropy manifest themselves.

Now, with the basic premise of evolution and the "scientific" study of the origin of life we have a scientific concept—not even a legitimate theory—suspending the very laws of science. A big bang by the very laws of science, no matter how *big,* can never create anything. Additionally, according to the law of inertia the rotation of the planets spinning off from the big bang should be conserved, spinning the same direction. At the very least, the moons of planets should be orbiting in the same direction. This, however, is not the case. The best answer provided to support this absurdity of logic and scientific reason is that certain scientists have claimed that they are allowed to exercise sovereignty over the laws of science when they deem appropriate. I am not making this up. So, the best scientists today now claim that they can do something while they ridicule others for believing in a God that can do that very same thing. I began to look with skepticism at some of the things I was taught in school in the name of "science."

> *Despite the fact that the Bible was apparently written by mere men, so were all of my science texts.*

Back to my attempt at tearing apart the Bible. As I read it, I began to pay attention to what it said about itself, about the nature and being of mankind, and about the natural world. Despite the fact that this book was apparently written by mere men, so were all of my science texts. Applying the scientific method as I had learned it, I began to find it impossible to invalidate the claims made in the pages of the Bible. Quite the opposite—I began to discover the origin of that common thread I observed in my scientific studies. The Bible clearly says that it is the perfect product of a perfect God using men to write as an engineer uses science to design. It was mere common sense, as an engineer, almost trivial to know that every design most assuredly has a designer. I could no longer ignore the fact that the "thumbprint" I observed throughout the fields of science was indeed the thumbprint of God. Now what?

I became what is generally termed a seeker. I was not seeking a group of people to hang out with or to socialize with. I was seeking the truth. I already had plenty of friends. I began studying the Bible as I had my texts. After receiving my Masters of Science degree in Aerospace Engineering systems design, I was still seeking the truth. No longer a self-admitted atheist, I was just an intellectually honest seeker of the truth. The Designer and Creator of everything did it all for a reason. The splendor of creation and the purpose of man were designed to bring glory and honor to their Creator. I think a sunset or a moon rise accomplish that task quite perfectly. Man, on the other hand, has failed to function as he was designed. That failure is not due to any flaw in the design—the design is perfect. The failures are due to man's own accord, as we continuously and willfully fail to meet the quality control standards set before us.

Finally, in April 1996, I heard the message of the truth and it made sense. I heard a pastor give a message on Matthew 18:21–35. I understood in an instant that I had knowingly failed to satisfy the requirements and purpose of my design. This failure is called sin. Despite that fact, the perfect Designer, the God of the Bible, had made provision to perfectly compensate. The quality control test is the Ten Commandments. The life of Jesus Christ showed me the design standard, perfection. The death of Jesus Christ made up for my failure of that standard. The resurrection of Jesus Christ gave proof and evidence for the effectiveness of God's plan to redeem any who would repent of their failure and have faith in the work accomplished in the life, death, and resurrection of Jesus Christ. That faith is like the faith you have when you go over a bridge and without concern fully expect to arrive on the other side. As any engineering student knows in studying the flaws of the Tacoma Narrows Bridge, bridges can let you down, but faith in Christ will never fail.

My spiritual rebirth gave substance to the reality of my regenerated heart and mind in the form of a true desire to live for my Creator and not for myself. Just like the physical world, our faith in the absolute truth and power of the God of the Bible will produce solid verifiable evidence. Paul summarized the science of faith superbly in Hebrews 11:1,6: "Now faith is the substance of things hoped for, the evidence of things not seen ... But without faith it is impossible to please Him, for he who comes to God must believe that He is, and that He is a rewarder of those who diligently seek Him."

Some of the substance and evidence in my own life is a true love for God's Word, a desire to live by that Word and not my own will, and several phone calls to some of those Christians I used to ridicule. After apologizing to them for my past attitude and comments, I informed them that they were indeed correct all along. I told them I had been born again. I encouraged them to never give up the faith.

Now I find myself the subject of mocking and ridicule by those who worship themselves and not their Creator. I encourage them to take the time to honestly investigate God's Word and to

assess if the real problem does not actually lie within their own egos.
To God be the glory!

14

WHY BOTHER?

"Give me a lever long enough and a fulcrum on which to place it, and I shall move the world."

—Archimedes

Throughout this book, my aim has not been to simply convince you that God exists. Every human ever born has an intellectual knowledge of God's existence through the evidence of creation, and has a moral knowledge of God via the conscience. In truth, you're not denying the existence of God, you're denying the voice of your conscience.

What I'm trying to convince you of is your terrible danger. Death is not part of evolution's unfolding plan. Death is God's payment for sin. Even if you manage to make it through to old age, you will die. You may die sick, or you may die healthy. But you will die. You may not be aware of it, but every year in the U.S. alone, around 90,000 people die in hospitals—from medical mistakes. That is, one American dies in a hospital from a medical error or a lethal infection every six minutes. Medical blunders are the eighth leading cause of death in the United

States. A horrifying 43,443 people died in car accidents in one year—one American is killed by a traffic accident every 12 minutes. That may make you want to stay home. Think again. One American is killed in an accident at home every 29 minutes—that's an annual total of over 18,000 deaths.

One is accidentally poisoned to death every 27 minutes (19,457). Falls killed 17,227 people back in 2004—that is, one every 31 minutes. One American is killed by a drunk driver every 31 minutes (16,885). Murders are down since the 1990s (unless Hollywood has succeeded in teaching more people how to disguise murder). One American is murdered every 32 minutes. According to the FBI, 17,034 people were murdered in 2006.[130] One more statistic to cheer you up: Every 30 seconds, a woman somewhere in the world gives birth to a child. She must be found and stopped.

The Bible makes it very clear that death is punishment for crimes committed against God, and physical death for the sinner is the doorway to damnation. If you despise the God who gave you every blessing, He will take every merciful blessing back and give you what you deserve: justice. Such a thought horrifies me. I can hardly entertain it in my mind. That's why I have devoted my life to warning this world that God means what He says. I don't *believe* Hell is a real place and that all who have sinned against God are going there. I *know* it's a reality. That's not arrogance. It's the truth.

I know that certain churches have used the threat of Hell to rule the masses, but that doesn't negate its reality. I know Hell is real because I have the greatest authority on this earth that tells me of it—the Word of God. I know this because the voice of reason tells me that God is just. I also know this because if God wasn't angry at sin (and sinners), the perfect Savior wouldn't have had to suffer in such a horrible way on the cross.

An atheist once told me that any person who believed what I believed would be running around the streets trying to warn people of Hell's existence. That's what I have been doing for more than 35 years. I have stood up on a soap box thousands of times and pleaded with people. I have given out hundreds of thousands of gospel tracts in the hope that people will read them and get right with God. I have spoken personally one-on-one to thousands of people, and I will continue pleading with people to repent and trust the Savior, as long as I am able to and still have breath in my lungs. I wouldn't do this if Hell didn't exist.

I am not only horrified at the thought of what will happen to the lost after this life, I am horrified at what happens to them in this life. Those who reject the gospel are left with nothing but futility. It is a night mare to have that revelation and not know God. Every pleasure you find in this life is transient. Sadly, it takes some people a lifetime to figure this out. I was able to come to this understanding by the age of 22 years. I realized that everything I held dear to me was going to be ripped from my hands by death. I began to understand that nothing I could see was eternal.

> *I am not only horrified at the thought of what will happen to the lost after this life, I am horrified at what happens to them in this life.*

Many people, as old age and death approach, sink into deep depression, and many even take their own lives. Consider these tragic words from people who think about life and its futility. William Shakespeare wrote, "Life is a tale told by an idiot, full of sound and fury, signifying nothing." Longfellow said, "Life is but an empty dream." Ernest Hemingway lamented, "Life is just a dirty trick, a short journey from nothingness to nothingness." Life was so empty for Hemingway that he took his own life. His father, two siblings, and granddaughter Margaux also found life futile and committed suicide. Samuel Becket said, "Life is an indefinite waiting for an explanation that never comes."

The "explanation" that never came to him is there for those who want to open the pages of the Bible, life's instruction Book. The Bible tells us why we live in futility and how to break out of it. Romans chapter 8 tells us that God subjected the entire fallen creation to futility, but there is a new world coming for those who trust in His mercy.

Jess the Agnostic

Recently I was making dinner for Sue when I tried cooking with oil for the first time. I poured about half an inch into the frying pan, turned the gas on, and dropped a piece of fish in. Suddenly I was staring at the two-foot flame roaring from the pan. It was then that I thought about the fire extinguisher that sat in the corner gathering dust. It was my dilemma that made me value it.

The gospel is a fire extinguisher that puts out the fire of God's wrath against our sins. Sadly, most people take little notice of the gospel, because they don't see their need. Thankfully, now and then, someone takes notice.

The following is a conversation between Todd Friel, host of The Way of the Master Radio program,[131] and Jess, an agnostic who called the program. Kirk Cameron and I had debated two atheists, Brain Sapient and "Kelly," on ABC about the existence of God, and after watching the debate Jess found the truths that we shared compelling.

Jess: The truth of the matter is, I guess I consider myself an agnostic. I wouldn't say that I don't believe in God because especially lately

I can't really deny that there isn't a God. The things that Kirk and Ray said, ... I don't know why, it made sense to me—what they said about my conscience. It's something that I could not deny. The fact of the matter is, if there is a Supreme Being, and if there is a law that people are supposed to live by and if there is a Hell, for some reason lately I've been thinking I'm going there. I can't shake it, I don't know. And I wasn't too impressed about those people that you guys were debating. If that's what an atheist is ... You know the way that they are—they're very disrespectful and they seem very self-centered. I've lived that way and that's the reason why I have the guilt that I have right now, because the way I've lived my life has been in total disregard for other people around me; just a self-centered lifestyle.

And now that I look around me, the people that I've hurt, if there was something in my life for me to be held accountable for ... I would have been spared a lot of heartache; not just me but a lot of other people. And it's not just me, I've been talking to a lot of people—my family. And I tell you, my family hasn't been doing too great. And we've been living without any religion in our lives. That's all we've ever known, you know?

Todd: So, Jess, you heard them talking about the conscience and the commandments and judging yourself by the standard that God has given to us—the Ten Commandments. And so, you've explained everything really swell ... what has God done so that you don't have to go to Hell?

Jess: That's the thing I can't get over, you know? People say that He died for my sins?

Todd: Yeah.

Jess: But I should be feeling all better about it, but for some reason I don't.

Todd: Well, it's because your sins haven't been forgiven yet. Acknowledging that He died for your sins doesn't get you saved. Learning about Him and going, *Oh, okay, that's how it works; that's interesting,* and not responding to it will leave you in the same place you were before you heard about it. Okay? So, this is kind of a pathetic analogy but it's like, if money is in the bank, you have to access the money to get it out. It doesn't do you any good to believe, *Oh! There's a million dollars in the bank with my name on it? Oh, that's nice.* But you never go into the bank and you never access it. The same thing is true with forgiveness. Forgiveness is available but you must respond to the good news of the gospel, Jess. And the way that you respond biblically, that will allow you to be forgiven by God so that He will save you, is through repentance and faith. Okay?

Jess: Yeah.

Todd: Now, there's two types of repentance, Jess. And I'm sharing this with you, not to dump theology on you, but because you said something kind of interesting. You said that you've been looking at life and it hasn't been turning out so swell. And...

Jess: Oh yeah, and it's not just that. I'll tell you something ... I know I have the power to make life as swell as I want it, but the fact of the matter is, I'll hurt a lot of people doing it.

Todd: Well, see, but the least of your concerns is how bad life is or what the consequences have been. You see, if you say that you're sorry to God because of the mistakes that you've made and the consequences and the heartache that it's caused other people—that's not biblical repentance. That's being sorry for the consequences.

Jess: The way I've been seeing things lately, I don't care if I'm living at the shelter. If I'm right with God, that's all I want.

Todd: There you go! Okay then, Jess, here's what you need to do. You need to, if you will, not call me, you need to call God and basically tell Him everything that you've just shared with me. That's what repentance is: *I've blown it! I've acted wrongly. I've done everything in rebellion against You. I was an idiot. I was a fool. I am sorry! I don't want to live that way any more. Have mercy on me. Please forgive me. I trust in Jesus Christ for my eternity.* That is repentance and that is putting your faith in Jesus Christ. And the Bible promises if you will do that,

Jess, God will forgive all of your sins; He will make you His child and grant you everlasting life.

Jess: So I guess I've got to get me one of those. I've been reading the Bible online. You can find it online, it's there for anyone who wants to read it. And I've been trying to read it.

Todd: Before you go, just hold on—we'll send you a Bible that you can read, and it will be simple and will have all kinds of good stuff in there for you. So we'll get you a Bible. But right now you know everything you need to know. Reading the Bible doesn't get you saved either.

Jess: All right.

Todd: All right? Trying to do good from now on, that doesn't get you saved either. Here's the deal, Jess: God died on a cross to forgive your sins so that He could save you totally, completely, fully, so that He can get all of the credit for it. You reading the Bible or doing good things, if you do that then you earn some of your forgiveness and that's not the way it works. You can't earn your forgiveness; it is a gift of God so that only He can take the credit for it so that you can't boast. So, Jess, here's what I'd like you to do, all right? I'm going to give you an assignment. Here's what I want you to think about, Jess; this is the "formula," if you will, for getting right with God.

Jess: Yup.

Todd: And it sounds like you've done a lot of this: think about the Ten Commandments, think about looking with lust...

Jess: I don't even know what they are, really, I mean I don't have them memorized. I've looked at them but...

Todd: Well, all right, here you go. Are you ready? Has God been first in your life, every day, every minute?

Jess: Absolutely not. I've been first in my life.

Todd: Yeah, that's right. Have you've made a graven image of your god by saying that he's like this or like that or that he maybe doesn't exist?

Jess: I've been questioning a lot about God and I've been questioning His existence, so, you know...

Todd: All right. So you've made an idol too. Have you ever taken His name in vain?

Jess: Oh, yeah.

Todd: Yeah. Have you set aside a day for God every week?

Jess: No.

Todd: Were you a perfect child? Did you obey your parents every time they told you what to do?

Jess: No.

Todd: All right. Have you murdered anybody?

Jess: No.

Todd: Well, that's good, but here's the problem. God's judgment goes well beyond what we do. It goes into our thought life. So, Jess, have you ever been really angry at somebody, flipped them off, called them a nasty name?

Jess: The way you described it, I'm a mass-murderer, man.

Todd: There you go; just like the rest of us. All right—adultery?

Jess: Well, you know, I've been in a relationship for a long time but we aren't married, so I don't know...

Todd: Okay, well, there's a difference. That's fornication. But here it gets even worse, Jess. Jesus said that if you just look at a woman with lust you've committed adultery in your heart. So, Jess, it's not just committing the act physically, it's just thinking about it and God knows it and sees you as an adulterer at heart. Have you ever stolen anything?

Jess: Yup.

Todd: Uh huh. Have you ever lied?

Jess: Oh, yeah.

Todd: Have you ever wanted something that didn't belong to you—want to win the lottery, want that car, just really desired things?

Jess: I play the lottery every day.

Todd: There you go. Okay, there are the Ten Commandments, Jess. You broke all ten of them just like the rest of us. You're going to die. You're going to stand before God. What should He do to you, Jess?

Jess: Like I said, I've been saying it all along—I belong down under, wherever that place is.

Todd: All right.

Jess: If it's there, I know I'm going. And that's the thing about it. That's probably the biggest thing at that debate that made sense to me ... I couldn't deny it...

Todd: Now, what did Jesus do to prove His love and to rescue you?

Jess: He gave His life.

Todd: Died on a cross...

Jess: Died on a cross...

Todd: ... got beaten and whooped, gagged for air, died on a cross for you so that you can be forgiven if you'll repent and put your trust in Him. So, I'm going to put you on hold. We're going to grab your address so we can send you a Bible, Jess. You need to think about your sins; think about Jesus dying on the cross for you; and then call out to Him. Okay?

Jess: All right.

Todd: And then start reading your Bible like nobody's business and do what it says. But you'll have a new attitude about it, Jess. You'll want to read the Bible because that's where Jesus is talked about. That's where He's described and you'll just want to learn more about Him, but first you've got to be in a right relationship with Him. Think about your sins; think about the Savior. That's the combination and, Jess, we're going to be praying for you like nobody's business. We can't save you; there's nothing we can do. We can't have you say a prayer. You've got to talk to God. Okay?

Jess: Well, thanks.

Todd: All right, I'm glad you called us. I realize what this takes to do this...

Jess: Well, thanks for taking the time, man.

He Grabbed the Horns!

I am so honored that you picked up this book, and that you read it. Perhaps you did so out of curiosity, or because you couldn't believe that a klutz like me could write a book. Whatever the case, please don't stop here. Pick up a Bible and begin reading it as though your life depended on it. Do what Todd Friel told Jess to do. Think about your sins, then think about the Savior. And like Todd said to Jess, I will be praying for you like nobody's business. There's good reason for that. Your salvation doesn't depend on the fact that you know God exists. It depends on your knowing Him personally. Jesus said, "And this is eternal life, *that they may know You*, the only true God, and Jesus Christ whom You have sent" (John 17:3, emphasis added). So please, of all things you do in this short life, make sure that you *know* Him.

Once you *do* know Him, you have a compelling reason to tell others about Him.

In August 2007, Kirk and I finished a shoot for the third season of our television program. It was called "Where Has the Passion Gone?" and looked at why we have lost passion in our preaching. The teaching is based on a portion of

Scripture where King Saul threatened to cut a yoke of oxen in pieces. As we spoke, we stood behind a small bull that had a big hump on its back and long horns.

When the filming was over, for some reason, I asked the cowboy who was holding the animal if it could be ridden. Moments later, I quietly slipped onto its back. Suddenly the bull took off, and I instinctively grabbed the horns. The "ride" lasted for only a few seconds. The amusing thing wasn't me on a bull, but that Kirk was incredulous at what he had just seen. He kept saying, "He grabbed the horns! He grabbed the horns!" He said it four times.

My justification for taking the bull by the horns was that I had no choice. There was no rope around the beast's belly for me to grab, and the only other choice was its ears, and I'm not *that* stupid. Sure.

> The world speaks more about Hell than the Church does. Most of the contemporary Church is afraid to even mention the word.

So why did I (an intelligent, clear-thinking human being) get onto the back of a bull? It was because I had been standing with it for about thirty minutes and I knew that I had some sort of authority over it. Strong though it was, when it had gotten spooked a couple of times during filming, I was able to pull it back into position.

So when I got onto the animal, I had that knowledge tucked into my mind. Of course, I could have been gored by its horns, but I didn't think too deeply about it, because if I wanted to ride the bull, I had to take the risk.

While I risk being "gored" by atheists for writing this book, I have a great motivation to do so. *People are going to Hell, and they must be warned.* If there was no Hell, I wouldn't bother pouring my heart out to strangers I meet, and each Saturday afternoon passionately preaching open-air at the base of the Huntington Beach pier. If there was no Hell, like the rest of this world, I would get on with my own life and the pursuit of happiness.

In our program script, Kirk and I talk about the fact that the world speaks more about Hell than the Church does. They casually use phrases like *all Hell broke loose, like a bat out of Hell, there will be Hell to pay, just for the Hell of it,* and someone being *as mad as a Hell.* When something is hopeless, they say *he doesn't have a hope in Hell.* Then there's *the road to Hell,* which is paved with good intentions, *come Hell or high water, until Hell freezes over.* They casually speak of how certain Hell is, with *as sure as Hell,* and of course, when they are angry, they tell each other to *go to Hell.*

In contrast, most of the contemporary Church (which is commanded to "warn" every man) is afraid to even *mention* the word, for fear of offending the world.

Think about the rich man of whom Jesus spoke. Much to his horror, he died and found himself in Hell, and being in torments and anguish of soul he pleaded with Abraham to send Lazarus to speak to his loved ones—"that he may testify to them, *lest they come to this place of torment*" (Luke 16:28).

Lately, in an effort to help awaken sinners, I have resorted to asking if they like it when their dentist's drill hits a raw nerve. No one does. I tell them that God is so angry at sin, He says that He will give them "tribulation and anguish" forever (see Romans 2:9). "Anguish" is a word we rarely use. The dentist's drill hitting a raw nerve is called "acute pain." It's not up there with "anguish." Forgive the dreadful analogy, but "anguish" is perhaps the word used to describe the emotion of a loving parent who finds his beloved little daughter lying dead at the bottom of a swimming pool.

We live in an insane world. God offers the lost everlasting life through the gospel, and they argue about it. They resist Heaven as though it were Hell itself. He offers them "pleasure forevermore," and they choose "anguish" for eternity. But if we love them, we must overcome our fears and plead with a sin-loving world to repent and turn to the Savior. If you are a Christian, if the love of God dwells within you, you have no choice. Please, while there is still time—take a risk, and grab the bull by the horns.

END NOTES

[1] Brian Braiker, "God's Numbers," March 31, 2007 <www.msnbc.msn.com/id/17879317/site/newsweek>.

[2] Kenneth R. Miller, Ph.D., and Joseph Levine, Ph.D., *Biology* (Upper Saddle River, NJ: Prentice Hall, 2002), p.15.

[3] Sir Isaac Newton, *The Mathematical Principles of Natural Philosophy*, Book III, Andrew Motte, trans. (London: H.D. Symonds, 1803), pp.310–314 <www.thenagain.info/Classes/Sources/Newton.html.>.

[4] Max Jammer, *Einstein and Religion: Physics and Theology* (Princeton: Princeton University Press, 1999), p.97.

[5] Denis Brian, *Einstein: A Life* (New York: John Wiley and Sons, 1996), p.186.

[6] Friedrich Dürrenmatt, *Albert Einstein* (Zürich, 1979).

[7] Brian, *Einstein: A Life*, p.119.

[8] Robert Jastrow, "Evolution: Selection for perfection," *Science Digest*, December 1981, p.86.

[9] Riccardo Levi-Setti, *Trilobites* (Chicago: University of Chicago Press, 1993), pp.57–58.

[10] Charles Darwin, *On the Origin of Species* (London: J.M. Dent & Sons Ltd., 1971), p.167.

[11] Ernst Mayr, interview with Edge <www.edge.org/3rd_culture/mayr/mayr_index.html>.

[12] "What Is Evolution?" <http://atheism.about.com/library/FAQs/evo/blfaq_evo_science.htm>.

[13] Andrei Linde, "The Self-Reproducing Inflationary Universe," *Scientific American*, vol.271, November 1994, p.54.

[14] "Telescope Detects Space Dust," October 10, 2007 <www.cnn.com/2007/TECH/space/10/10/cosmic.dust.ap/index.html>.

[15] Linda Vu, "Spitzer Helps Solve Mystery of Space Dust," NASA Jet Propulsion Laboratory, June 8, 2006 <www.jpl.nasa.gov/news/features.cfm?feature=1117>.

[16] Charles Darwin, letter to a Dutch student at the University of Utrecht, April 2, 1873, *The Life and Letters of Charles Darwin* (London: John Murray, 1888), p.306.

[17] Stephen Hawking, *Austin American-Statesman*, October 19, 1997.

[18] Sir Fred Hoyle and Chandra Wickramasinghe, *Evolution from Space*

(New York: Simon & Schuster, 1984), p.148.
[19] Michael Denton, *Evolution: A Theory in Crisis* (Bethesda, MD: Adler & Adler, 1986), p.250.
[20] Jeffrey Bada, "Life's Crucible," *Earth*, February 1998, p.40 <www.darwinismrefuted.com/molecular_biology_08.html>.
[21] *Washington Post* online forum, September 26, 2001 <http://discuss.washingtonpost.com/wp-srv/zforum/01/evolution2_092601.htm>.
[22] Kids Genetics, GlaxoSmithKline <http://genetics.gsk.com/kids/dna01.htm>.
[23] Denton, *Evolution: Theory in Crisis*.
[24] "Genome Facts," Nova Online <www.pbs.org/wgbh/nova/genome/facts.html>.
[25] Charles B. Thaxton, Ph.D., "DNA, Design and the Origin of Life," November 13–16, 1986 <www.origins.org/articles/thaxton_dnadesign.html#ref15>.
[26] Steven Swinford, "I've found God, says man who cracked the genome," June 11, 2006 <www.timesonline.co.uk/tol/news/uk/article673663.ece>.
[27] Rich Deem, "One Flew Over the Cuckoo's Nest?" <www.god-andscience.org/apologetics/flew.html>.

[28] Janet Folger, "Huckabee was right," June 12, 2007 <www.worldnetdaily.com/news/article.asp?ARTICLE_ID=56123>.

[29] David A. Dewitt, Ph.D., "Chimp Genome Sequence Very Different From Man," September 5, 2005 <www.answersingenesis.org/docs2005/0905chimp.asp>.

[30] Don Batten, "Human/chimp DNA Similarity," *Creation,* vol.19, iss.1, December 1996, pp.21–22 <www.answersingenesis.org/creation/v19/i1/dna.asp>.

[31] Steve Jones, interview on *The Science Show,* broadcast on ABC Radio, January 1, 2002 <www.abc.net.au/rn/science/ss/stories/s456478.htm>.

[32] Pierre-Paul Grassé, *Evolution of Living Organisms* (New York: Academic Press, 1977), p.82.

[33] Charles Darwin, *On the Origin of Species* (London: John Murray, 1872), pp.133–134.

[34] Christopher P. Sloan, "Feathers for T. rex?" *National Geographic,* vol.196, no.5, November 1999, pp.99–105.

[35] Storrs L. Olsen, Open letter to Dr. Peter Raven, Secretary, National Geographic Society, November 1, 1999 <www.true-origin.org/birdevoletter.asp>.

[36] "Understanding Evolution For Teachers," University of California Museum of Paleontology <http://evolution.berkeley.edu/evosite/lines/IAtransitional.shtml>.

[37] Alexander Williams and Jonathan Sarfati, "Not at all like a whale," *Creation*, vol.27, iss.2, March 2005, pp.20–22 <www.answersingenesis.org/creation/v27/i2/whale.asp>.

[38] Mary Lord, "The Piltdown Chicken: Scientists eat crow over so-called missing link," *U.S. News & World Report*, February 14, 2000 <http://www.usnews.com/usnews/culture/articles/000214/archive_032798.htm>.

[39] Richard Leakey, in a PBS documentary, 1990 <www.wasdarwinright.com/earlyman-f.htm>.

[40] Boyce Rensberger, "Ideas on Evolution Going Through a Revolution Among Scientists," *Houston Chronicle*, November 5, 1980, sec.4, p.15.

[41] Stephen Gould, *The Panda's Thumb* (New York: W.W. Norton, 1980), pp.181, 189.

[42] T.S. Kemp, *Fossils and Evolution* (New York: Oxford University Press, 1999), p.253.

[43] Robert L. Carroll, *Patterns and Processes of Vertebrate Evolution* (New York: Cambridge University Press, 1997), p.9.
[44] Richard Dawkins, *The Blind Watchmaker* (New York: W.W. Norton Co., 1987), pp.229–230.
[45] Ibid.
[46] "Evolution of Turtles," *Encyclopedia Britannica*, vol.26 (Encyclopedia Britannica Pub., 1986), p.750.
[47] Stephen J. Gould, "The Return of Hopeful Monsters," *Natural History*, vol.86, June/July 1977, p.28.
[48] Roger Lewin, "Evolutionary Theory Under Fire," *Science*, vol.210, November 21, 1980, p.884.
[49] Lee Spetner, *Not by Chance* (Brooklyn, NY: The Judaica Press Inc.), pp.131–132.
[50] "Understanding Evolution," University of California Museum of Paleontology <http://evolution.berkeley.edu/evolibrary/article/0_0_0/mutations_07>.
[51] Ibid.
[52] Soren Lovtrup, *Darwinism: The Refutation of a Myth* (Beckingham, Kent: Croom Helm Ltd., 1987), p.275.
[53] Stephen Jay Gould, "Not Necessarily a Wing," *Natural History*, October 1985, pp.12–13.

[54] Michael Denton, interview with Access Research Network, 2005 <www.arn.org/docs/orpages/or152/dent.htm>.

[55] Roger Lewin, "Evolutionary Theory Under Fire," *Science*, vol.210, November 21, 1980, p.883.

[56] Denton, interview with Access Research Network.

[57] "Understanding Evolution," University of California Museum of Paleontology <http://evolution.berkeley.edu/evolibrary/article/0_0_0/mutations_07>.

[58] Lovtrup, *Darwinism: The Refutation of a Myth*, p.422.

[59] Horatio Hackett Newman, quoted in *The World's Most Famous Court Trial: The Tennessee Evolution Case* (Dayton, TN: Bryan College, 1925, reprinted 1990), p.268.

[60] Richard Dawkins, *The Humanist*, vol.57, no.1, January/February 1997 <www.thehumanist.org/humanist/articles/dawkins.html>.

[61] *Vintage Muggeridge* (William B. Eerdmans Publishing Company, 1981), p.41.

[62] Richard Dawkins <www.positiveatheism.org/hist/quotes/dawkins.htm>.

[63] Richard Dawkins, interview with Lanny Swerdlow (Portland, Oregon, 1996).

[64] Richard Dawkins, "Book Review" (of Donald Johanson and Maitland Edey's *Blueprint), The New York Times,* sec.7, p.3, April 9, 1989.

[65] Henry M. Morris and Gary E. Parker, *What is Creation Science?* (El Cajon, CA: Master Books, 1987).

[66] Michael Ruse, "Darwin's Theory: An Exercise in Science," *New Scientist,* June 25, 1981, p.828.

[67] Jerry Bergman, "Darwin Skeptics," September 11, 2006 <www.rae.org/darwinskeptics.html>.

[68] Dr. Francis Collins, interview with Jon Sweeny, 2007 <www.explore faith.org/speaking_collins.html>.

[69] Dave Miller, "Most Americans Still Reject Evolution," October 2007 <www.apologeticspress.org/articles/3477>.

[70] Freeman J. Dyson, cited in Barrow and Tipler, *Anthropic Cos mo logical Principle* (New York: Oxford University Press, 1988), p.318.

[71] Arno Penzias, quoted by D.L. Brock in *Our Universe: Accident or Design* (Wits, S. Africa: Star Watch, 1992), p.42.

[72] Fred Hoyle, *The Intelligent Universe* (London: Michael Joseph, 1983), p.220.

[73] ABC's "Nightline" with Ted Koppel, April 24, 1992.

[74] Bertrand Russell, *Religion and Science* (New York: Oxford University Press, 1997), p.14.

[75] Richard Feynman, *The Character of Physical Law* (Cambridge, MA: MIT Press, 1967), p.77.

[76] Douglas Theobald, Ph.D., "29+ Evidences for Macro evolution," 2006 <www.talkorigins.org/faqs/comdesc/sciproof.html>.

[77] H.P. Yockey, "A calculation of the probability of spontaneous bio genesis by information theory," *Journal of Theoretical Biology*, vol.67, 1977, p.396.

[78] Paul Davies, *The Edge of Infinity* (New York: Simon & Schuster, 1981), p.161.

[79] Michael Denton, *Evolution: A Theory in Crisis* (Bethesda, MD: Adler & Adler, 1986).

[80] James Shapiro, "In the Details ... What?" *National Review*, September 19, 1996, pp.62–65.

[81] Voltaire, *The Works of Voltaire, Vol.4* (New York: E.R. DuMont, 1901).

[82] Antony Flew, interview with Dr. Benjamin Wike, October 30, 2007 <www.tothesource.org/10_30_2007/10_30_2007.htm>.

[83]   Theodore Roszak, *Unfinished Animal* (Harpercollins, 1975), pp.101–102.

[84]   Robin Marantz Henig, "Darwin's God," *The New York Times*, March 4, 2007 <www.nytimes.com/2007/03/04/magazine/04evolution.t.html?pagewanted=1>.

[85]   Ibid.

[86]   Brian Braiker, "God's Numbers," March 31, 2007 <www.msnbc.msn.com/id/17879317/site/newsweek>.

[87]   CIA World Factbook 2007 <www.cia.gov/library/publications/the-world-factbook/fields/2122.html>.

[88]   Henig, "Darwin's God."

[89]   *Online Etymology Dictionary*, Douglas Harper, historian <http://dictionary.reference.com/browse/conscience>.

[90]   "Two Australian girls given life for murder experiment," May 19, 2007 <http://uk.reuters.com/article/worldNews/idUKSYD28706220070510>.

[91]   Proverbs 12:22.

[92]   Matthew 5:27,28.

[93]   1 John 3:15.

[94]   Frank Newport, "Americans More Likely to Believe in God Than the Devil, Heaven More Than Hell," June 13, 2007 <www.gallup.com/poll/27877/Americans-

More-Likely-Believe-God-Than-Devil-Heaven-More-Than-Hell.aspx>.

[95] Matthew 12:36.

[96] A condensed version of this chapter, called *Why Christianity?*, is available in booklet form. See www.livingwaters.com.

[97] See Psalm 111:10.

[98] "Is it possible for a man to be reborn as a lower animal?" Maharshi: "Yes. It is possible, as illustrated by Jada Bharata—the scriptural anecdote of a royal sage having been reborn as a deer" <www.hinduism.co.za/reincarn.htm>.

[99] "When you transcend your thinking mind in the realization of your own pure, timeless, ever-present awareness, then the illusion of time completely collapses, and you become utterly free of the samsaric cycle of time, change, impermanence, and suffering" <www.buddhistinformation.com>.

[100] "Then those whose balance (of good deeds) is heavy, they will be successful. But those whose balance is light, will be those who have lost their souls; in hell will they abide" (Surah 23:102,103).

[101] "The sacrifice of the wicked is an abomination to the Lord, but the

prayer of the upright is His delight" (Proverbs 15:8).
[102] See Romans 13:14.
[103] Galatians 3:13.
[104] Romans 8:2.
[105] John 3:16.
[106] Richard Wurmbrand, *Proofs of God's Existence* (Bartlesville, OK: Living Sacrifice Books, 2007), p.72.
[107] See Romans 2:15.
[108] See Romans 4:15.
[109] Ezekiel 11:19,20.
[110] Ephesians 4:24.
[111] 2 Corinthians 5:17.
[112] John 1:12,13.
[113] Romans 1:16.
[114] John 16:13.
[115] Galatians 6:15.
[116] Romans 15:4.
[117] 1 John 3:14.
[118] Philippians 4:7.
[119] 1 Peter 1:8.
[120] John 3:3–7; 1 Peter 1:23.
[121] 2 Corinthians 5:17.
[122] John 16:14.
[123] Galatians 6:14.
[124] 1 Peter 2:2.
[125] These questions are compiled by Donald Morgan, "Bible Inconsistencies:

[126] *Great Lives, Great Deeds* (Reader's Digest, 1964), pp.185,186.

[127] Jeffery L. Sheler, "Is the Bible True?" *Reader's Digest,* June 2000, p.186.

[128] Jewish Antiquities xviii.33 (early second century) from F.F. Bruce, *Jesus and Christian Origins Outside the New Testament* (Grand Rapids: Eerdmans, 1974), p.37.

[129] Wernher von Braun, Letter to California State Board of Education, September 14, 1972 <www.creationsafaris.com/wgcs_4vonbraun.htm>.

[130] National Safety Council for 2006; National Vital Statistics Report for 2006; Home Safety Council for 2004; Mothers Against Drunk Driving for 2005; Department of Justice for 2004.

[131] The daily radio program can be heard at www.WayoftheMasterRadio.com.

(continued from previous page) Bible Contradictions?" <www.infidels.org/library/modern/donald_morgan/contradictions.html>.

RESOURCES

If you have not yet placed your trust in Jesus Christ and would like additional information, please feel free to visit www.livingwaters.com and check out our resources. The following items may be helpful to you:
- *The Evidence Bible*
- *God Doesn't Believe in Atheists*
- *How to Live Forever ... Without Being Religious*
- *Scientific Facts in the Bible*
- *What Hollywood Believes*
- *Intelligent Design vs. Evolution*
- *The Science of Evolution* (DVD)
- *The Case for Atheism* (DVD)
- *The Greatest Gamble* (DVD)
- "Intelligent Design vs. Evolution" board game

If you are a new believer, please read the following booklet, written just for you:
- *Save Yourself Some Pain*

For Christians

Please visit our website where you can sign up for our free monthly e-newsletter. To learn how to share your faith the way Jesus did, don't miss these helpful publications:
- *The Way of the Master* (our most important book)
- *What Did Jesus Do?*

- *Hell's Best Kept Secret*
- *How to Bring Your Children to Christ ... & Keep Them There*
- *The Way of the Master for Kids*
- *The Way of the Master Minute*
- *Gold Series: Spurgeon Gold, Whitefield Gold, Wesley Gold*
- *Thanks a Million! An Adventure in Biblical Evangelism*
- *How to Win Souls and Influence People*
- *Out of the Comfort Zone*

You can also gain further insights by listening to The Way of the Master Radio (www.WayoftheMasterRadio.com) and watching "The Way of the Master" television program (www.WayoftheMaster.com).

Also, please visit www.HollywoodandGod.com.

For a catalog of books, tracts, CDs, and DVDs by Ray Comfort, visit www.livingwaters.com, call 877-496-8688, or write to: Living Waters Publications, P.O. Box 1172, Bellflower, CA 90706.

The Evidence Bible

"*The Evidence Bible* is specially designed to rein force the faith of our times by offering hard evidence and scientific proof for the thinking mind."

—DR. D. JAMES KENNEDY

The Evidence Bible, based on more than two decades of research, has been commended by Josh Mc Dowell, Franklin Graham, Dr. Woodrow Kroll, and many other Christian leaders.
• Learn how to show the absurdity of evolution.
• See from Scripture how to prove God's existence without the use of faith.
• Discover how to prove the authenticity of the Bible through prophecy.
• See how the Bible is full of eye-opening scientific and medical facts.
• Read fascinating quotes from Darwin, Einstein, New ton, and other well-known scientists.

- Learn how to share your faith with your family, neighbors, and coworkers, as well as Muslims, Mormons, Jehovah's Witnesses, etc.
- Glean evangelistic wisdom from Charles Spurgeon, John Wesley, George Whitefield, D. L. Moody, John MacArthur, and many others.
- Discover answers to 100 common objections to Christianity.

Find out how to answer questions such as: Where did Cain get his wife? Why is there suffering? Why are there "contradictions" in the Bible? ... and much more!

School of Biblical Evangelism

Do you want to deepen your passion for the lost, for the cross, and for God? Then look no further. Join more than 9,000 students from around the world in the School of Biblical Evangelism, to learn how to witness and defend the faith.

With 101 lessons on subjects ranging from basic Christian doctrines to knowing our enemy, from false conversions to proving the deity of Jesus, you will be well-equipped to answer questions as you witness to anyone. This study course will help you to prove the authenticity of the Bible, provide ample evidence for creation, refute the claims of evolution, understand the beliefs of those in cults and other religions, and know how to reach both friends and strangers with the gospel.

"*A phenomenal course.*"

—Jim Culver

"*Awesome ... This course should be required in every theological seminary.*"

—Spencer S. Hanley

"*As a graduate of every other evangelism course I can find, yours by far has been the best.*"

—Bill Lawson

"*I have never seen anything as powerful as the teaching in the School of Biblical Evangelism.*"

—James W. Smith

Join online at www.biblicalevangelism.com or, to obtain the entire course in book form, call **800-437-1893** or visit fine bookstores everywhere

BACK COVER MATERIAL

With a recent wave of books on atheism becoming *New York Times* best-sellers, the God debate is heating up. Because of the implications, it's the most significant question of all time: *Is there a God, or isn't there?*

In this compelling book, Ray Comfort argues the case with simple logic and common sense. If there is a God, surely He has made His presence known so that anyone — young or old, scholar or schoolchild — can find Him.

By applying basic logic to three clear evidences for the existence of God, Comfort will help you to:

- Examine the case for evolution and see what top scientists are really saying about the theory
- Explore the facts that led the world's most notorious atheist to acknowledge a Creator theory
- Investigate the evidence to discover who God is

More than just thought-provoking, this book will convince you that belief in God is reasonable and rational — a matter of fact and not faith. Through 100% scientific proof, you can *know* that God exists.

RAY COMFORT is a best-selling author and co-host (with Kirk Cameron) of the awarding-winning TV program "The Way of the Master." Comfort was a platform speaker at the American Atheists Inc. National Convention and, along with Cameron, debated atheists on ABC's "Nightline." He is the author of more than 60 books, including *The Evidence Bible* (a Gold Medallion Award finalist) and *The Way of the Master*. He and his wife, Sue, live in Southern California, where they have three grown children.

www.ingramcontent.com/pod-product-compliance
Lightning Source LLC
Chambersburg PA
CBHW011742220426
43665CB00023B/2901